The Case for
Clarity, Compassion & Contentment

FINDING YOUR
CENTER

The Case for
Clarity, Compassion & Contentment

FINDING YOUR
CENTER

KIM PERONE

Center4C Publishing
BURNT HILLS, NEW YORK

Center4C Publishers
801 Route 50
Burnt Hills, NY 12027
www.center4c.com

This publication is not intended as a substitute
for the advice of health care professionals.

Cover design by Jennifer McDonald
Book design by Jessika Hazelton

Printed in the United States of America
The Troy Book Makers · Troy, New York · thetroybookmakers.com

To order additional copies of this title,
contact your favorite local bookstore
or visit www.shoptbmbooks.com

ISBN: 978-1-614684-879

Dedicated to
my husband Dave,
my heavenly son Jack,
and my earthly son Steven,
along with all the clients who have
blessed me as their
coach

"If you knew who walks beside you
on the path you have chosen,
fear would be impossible."

A COURSE IN MIRACLES

Contents

INTRODUCTION

Making the Case for Clarity, Compassion & Contentment

What a glorious four-year journey of clarity, compassion and contentment for us! However, this title, born as my business partner and fellow Life Coach, Helene Verdile, and I crafted a business plan for a life-coaching practice and wellness center, is much more than our business name. It's also indicative of what we feel so strongly about sharing with others as life coaches and what we offer clients, guests, and other practitioners who grace our shared space. This book, ***The Case for Clarity, Compassion, and Contentment,*** describes the three pillars we believe are so vital to living well.

If ever there was a time to stop and reflect on these qualities, it is now. Getting clear about our life's purpose, growing in compassion, and achieving contentment allows us to live our best lives and operate from our highest selves. Today, achieving these qualities and practicing them daily can be difficult for many reasons: the pace and pressure of modern life; false measures of success and unfavorable comparisons; and confusing messages we hear daily from family, friends, and society. Having made a business of living well and sharing these pillars with clients, workshop participants, event audiences, and employees in workplace training programs, my business partner and I regularly practice these principles, returning to them over and over again to stay focused on our goals and follow our true north.

I will admit, in crafting the name of our business four years ago, I imagined people hearing it and saying (out loud or in their heads), *"Yes, I want some of that!"* I know I wanted lots of all three! In 2014, we set upon our path as life coaches and building our plan, and in 2015 we opened our doors. During the past four years we have heard many confirm that these three words matter.

As we guide clients toward these three qualities in their lives, it is as if a 100-pound bag they have been dragging around has been lifted off their back. We all experience stress that may cause us to question ourselves, feel lack, and wander off personal course. But when we look at our lives using these pillars, we can see how magnificent we are and how amazing life is. This book is aimed at lifting the weight of the world off of you, sharing the premise of our center, and spreading our message of hope for a vibrant, meaningful, intentional life.

Our "Why"

Our culture flows with an undercurrent of stress, overwhelm, worry, anxiety, hurt, and anger. This counterculture, *which we may perceive as the actual culture,* contains the following sentiments (as well as many more!):

If I'm not worried, I'm not being responsible.

If I'm not stressed and busy, I'm lazy.

If I'm not angry at the opposition, I am not taking a stand.

If I don't have a lot of stuff or money, I am not worthy.

If a person is bad or wrong, it is not right to be compassionate toward him or her.

These statements are false and they represent limiting beliefs that represent the ego (false self) rather than our being (true self). We are not what we do. We are not how busy we are. We are not what we stand for, or how successful we are. Rather, we are whole beings who do not need to judge others to determine their worth nor make ourselves feel more worthy. We are worthy of love. We are on this earth for a purpose, but it is highly likely that it is not the purpose we think.

Our being is love. Our being is whole.

Our being has purpose.

Our worth is unconditional.

The Center for Clarity, Compassion & Contentment is more than a place; it is a movement of wellness, wholeness, and empowerment. While The Center is located in Saratoga County, New York, *the true "center" is in you.* We hope these pages help you tap into your own potential in new and deeper ways, and help you find your center, even in the frenzy of this world. We hope you use these pillars regularly to create peace in your life. Our tagline is "Find your center at our center," but in this book, we take a big leap out of the building. This book, and its companion, *Inspired Life Journal,* written by Helene, aim to create a framework for you to use to find empowerment.

Those who embrace clarity, compassion, and contentment not only live more satisfied and fulfilled lives, but also become mentors to others and make a difference in our world. We welcome you to consider the many ways you are a loving presence in the lives of others. Take a dive into these pages and cultivate even more clarity, compassion, and contentment in your own life than exists today. Understand that in doing so, you are opening the door for others to do so as well. My hope is that as you read these pages and work with the journal to answer questions, you conclude with a greater sense of self. Your clarity, your ability to meet everyone (including yourself) with compassion, and your achievement of a deeper sense of contentment—returning to these pillars over and over again as life tosses you about—is a superpower!

Living with clarity, compassion, and contentment means letting go of chaos and distress, any sense of victimhood, limiting beliefs, creating new measures for authentic success, and shifting paradigms for your betterment. Often it means honoring your own truth above the messaging of society. This can be hard work, but the result is an amazing journey of the soul. As you bravely peel off the layers of society's expectations and find your true self, you will be able to move toward a life you desire and that has purpose. *When clarity, compassion, and contentment are present, an inspired life is possible. The Case for Clarity, Compassion and Contentment*, together with Helene's *Inspired Life Journal,* is the collective book we *all* write together. This is only the beginning . . . .

Many blessings,

Kim Perone

CHAPTER 1

Clarity

*"For me the greatest beauty
always lies in the greatest clarity."*
—Gotthold Ephraim Lessing

In a crisis, we get clear in a hurry. But do we need a crisis to get clear? The sense of urgency prompts us to find our compass, settle on some focal points, and head in a direction, whether short term or long term. Or we may be extremely clear about what we want in life, but we encounter a particular challenge that requires us to alter our perspective. After a period of time feeling confused, we establish clarity moving forward. Yes, crisis works by providing a spark. But I say, let's not wait for a crisis to establish clarity.

In my own life, I was pretty clear that I wanted marriage, kids, and a career. I was extremely blessed to have achieved it all, and by age thirty, I was on top of the world. I had a handsome husband, two beautiful boys, ages five and three, and had just landed my dream job.

That precious world was shattered five years later. My need to reestablish clarity began with crisis: the death of my nine-year-old son, Jack, on September 4, 2004, four days after a terrible car accident launched a sequence of events that ended my life as I knew it. I was entering a terrifying new world. At thirty-five years old, I stood on the edge of a cliff looking over a vast chasm, unable to see the other side, but knowing I needed to get there. I needed sanity. I needed to stay sane for my surviving seven-year-old son, Steven. I was beyond blessed that he survived the car accident, and he deserved a good life. How I was going to give him a good life in the aftermath of this unfathomable loss was not clear.

Early on, I could see that Steve was looking to me for guidance on this terrifying path. He was watching me. He was watching us. If we were okay, he was okay. I desperately wanted him to feel safe, protected, and happy. My purpose soon became clear: give Steve a good life. We took family vacations, we had many sleepovers, we traveled with Steven's baseball team. We lived life with as much joy as possible. It seems so simple, but sometimes the simplest answers are the best ones.

Something amazing happened. He not only survived, he thrived. As Steven grew, he was always making those around him feel good. He developed a unique ability to be quiet and funny at the same time. When he was little, his physical humor entertained everyone. When he grew older, he became a soulful presence for his friends. He was a little brother to many, as Jack's friends all looked out for Steven and loved him as they did Jack.

We cannot get where we want to go without having a destination in mind. What we want out of life will guide our steps and dictate the actions we take.

As I share my message of hope with newly bereaved parents, I also share that finding clarity allowed me to achieve, to the best of my ability, a life of love and joy for Steve. It has been fourteen years since those unspeakable first days of shattering loss, and my precious son is now a wonderful and handsome young man of twenty-two who moved into his own apartment this year. I am so proud of how he has handled fear and loss with grace and dignity in his young life. I am deeply grateful for what he has taught me.

Loss, divorce, a medical diagnosis, or a brush with death can all lead us to clarity on what we want out of our lives. Our current day also calls for that level of clarity. Often the quiet whisper goes unnoticed. We gain clarity any time we choose, and we do not need to wait for some defining point or crisis in our lives to reach for it.

Instead, think about what is important to you? What are your values? Are you living these values, or are you living in opposition to these values? Are you constantly measuring your worth with someone else's standards? Are you seeing the world with others' expectations or putting your expectations onto others? Are you so exhausted or disappointed that you are unclear about what you care about? Is your mind occupied with yesterday and tomorrow, but never today?

Who are you?

If you've ever been asked this question, what do you say? I'll bet you mention your name, title, age, or job or family role in response. Have you ever heard anyone say, "I don't even know who I am anymore"? It's not because they forgot their name or who they are in relation to their personal relationships. Labels, roles, expectations, other people's images of who you are exist, and they get in the way of the better, more accurate, and sometimes impossible-to-articulate true self.

Who are you really? Not your name, not your height or weight. Not your role in life. While you may be a mother, father, sister, brother, daughter, son, this is not who you are. Neither are you your title or profession. Who you are transcends labels. You are a soul. You are a spiritual being, a divine extension of your creator, having a human experience. You are magnificent! So, are you honoring your magnificent self?

One way to determine who you are is to take some time to think about who you have always been, the part of you that has been consistent from the time you were little until now. What has been a common thread throughout your ages? This is your essence.

That essence, the real you, does not need labels. Are you honoring that self in your daily life?

Worthiness

How often do we feel like we need to earn our worth? Almost all the time! You were born with unconditional human worth; you do not need to earn your worthiness. This is not to imply that you do not need to work and take care of family, but it does mean that you, like every other human being, start life with a solid level of worthiness. As children, we may create a story around the need to perform to achieve love and worth. This can follow us throughout our lives, and we "put on a show" in order to feel worthy. Ultimately, this may drive us into misery, resentment, and exhaustion.

The reason the question of who we really are may be difficult to answer lies in a foundational lesson of life coaching. Our ego, which is part of our psyche, takes in information around us and tries to make sense of the world. This does not mean we are arrogant or self-absorbed, as the term is sometimes applied. This ego, while it does share traits such as self-importance, is a part of all of our minds. It is a problem-solving part of our brain, and one that wants to establish us as an individual, prove our worth, and protect us. It is the part of us that is fearful or worried. It is the part of us that gets offended and that judges others. It categorizes and perceives. It tells us there is always something to be done, achieved, accomplished.

This ego is considered the false self. It is the thinker, the voice in our head—and one that does not necessarily speak the truth. However, without getting clear on the ego's purpose, we believe we *are* those thoughts in our head, that we are our thinking. This part of our mind may keep us from joy because everything good is an expectation so it stops paying attention to the good in our lives and redirects its focus to thinking about problems and everything that is not going well. The ego serves a function, which we will take a closer look at in a moment, but it is extremely important that we understand it is a part of us, *not* the whole of us.

Our ego, or false self, is a function of our primal brain. We need it for survival. It enabled our ancestors to escape death because of a heightened ability to sense danger and live long enough to produce descendants. You are the descendant of the people who had the absolute best ability to sense danger. Hence, our modern-day problem is that when we sense danger, it is rarely true danger, as our ancestors experienced; we simply perceive a threat.

A difficult relative, an angry customer, an uncertain future—all trigger our sense of danger and light our fear, causing our brain to go into fight-or-flight mode. When our brain triggers this fight-or-flight response, a number of things happen: our vision sharpens, adrenaline and other chemicals flood the brain, and our amygdala (or primal brain) is activated. This is not the part of the brain that reasons well. The amygdala is the source of our instinct and it instigates the flow of chemicals that enable us to run from danger.

When I think of the amygdala, I imagine the movie *The Hunger Games*. In the movie's dystopian society, Katniss Everdeen needs to fight the other contestants for her life. Placed into the world of the game, she becomes the hunter and the hunted, and her heightened sense of danger enables her to survive.

In our daily lives, we don't need or want to be on that kind of alert. We want to operate in the parts of our brain that reason well and perform higher functions. All that adrenaline and norepinephrine flooding our system is intended to help us run fast (really fast!), but if we aren't running, it is just swirling in our system with no way to be expelled. Because of this, today we see countless stress-related ailments—literal physical illnesses. Rick Hanson, PhD, shares more about this on his website, RickHanson.net, which is full of books, blogs, and videos that help us understand what is happening in our brain when it's under stress.

Unlike the ego, our soul or being is our eternal or true self. This is the part of us that knows we are okay even in difficult situations. It is the part that knows we are connected to every other person. It is the part that sees only love rather than fear. The soul, our being, is beyond labels. Our true self is calm even when the world outside us is chaotic and unpredictable. Our soul is not concerned with avoiding challenges, but rather grows from challenges, changes, losses, and adversity.

We live with both the ego and the true self, and understanding them is a key to living at a higher level of consciousness. Knowing about these two selves allows us to become curious, instead of panicked, when something upsets us. We can use this knowledge to learn more about ourselves, rather than entertain an internal fight.

The Eternal Soul

My whole life, I have been aware of the concept of heaven: a beautiful, loving, completely safe place with God that we enter after we die. It was only after losing my son Jack that I began to realize that if heaven is where we go, it is where we come from as well.

Why did our soul come here? In the days, months, and years after losing Jack, I longed to know more. I had to become aware, for my sanity, that there was a bigger picture, even bigger than what I had learned. I thought about why I was here and why we had suffered such a devastating loss. I could not even survive without connecting with more tragedy. I read books about other parents who lost children, about orphans who lost their parents to AIDS in Africa, and about suffering in the Middle East. The images and stories from around the world of people suffering, in the same world I live in, allowed me to focus on moving forward one day at a time. My kinship with and compassion for others allowed me to focus on my purpose here. Perhaps an easy, breezy life was not the goal. I realized that I just happened to live in a part of the world that was quite comfortable and did not see much death and destruction. I started to connect with my journey and own it in a way that enabled me to live it very much on purpose. When it comes to understanding my true self, I can credit both of my sons for launching me into the search for a deeper truth.

Five years and eight days after we lost our beloved Jack, we lost my younger sister, Kristen, to cancer. Her eleven-month battle ended tragically. During that time, our family rallied to support Kristen, her baby, Owen, just four months old at the time of her diagnosis, and her husband, Omar. We had so much hope—after all, we had already lost Jack! We learned all too soon that one family tragedy did not prevent another.

Upon Kristen's passing and the months that followed, I struggled to reintegrate into my own life, grieve, and continue on with the same conviction as before. My conviction to give Steve a good life and stay sane and present for my loved ones now grew.

I don't think my anger, as part of the stages of grief, had even surfaced as part of my grieving for Jack, but when Kristen passed it came full force. I told my husband, "After losing Jack, I am so broken.... Now I am pissed!" I did not know who I felt worse for in my grief and empathy: my brother-in-law for losing his wife, my baby nephew for losing his mother, my parents for becoming bereaved as my husband and I were, or for Kristen for not being able to stay here and raise her baby. Or was this another form of pressure meant to return me to the fact that I was still crushed and processing my loss of Jack?

I was on my way to another breakdown, and this time it was raging, rather than heartbroken, and it involved both losses. There is no "getting over" the loss of a child, or anyone you love so deeply, but rather a weaving it into the fabric of our lives. I was still grieving Jack's loss (as I am still), and now I had my sister's devastating loss to incorporate into my life. My mantra "Stay sane and present for all who love me, and participate in giving these boys a good life" was newly strengthened.

Completely consumed with loss and distracted by thoughts of my motherless baby nephew in Connecticut with my amazing brother-in-law (now simply brother), and my own surviving son with me in New York, I realized they were both precious gifts in my world. But I was spending my limited energy at work and coming home with none left. I thought if there is *any* mother who knows she shouldn't be giving everything at the office, it surely was me, having lost a son already. I could not go back and redo time with Jack. If I knew I had only nine years with him, what would I have done differently?

From an intense need to focus on family and mental wellness, sprang intense clarity: I needed to leave my job and spend time at home with Steven, and give myself the freedom to travel to Connecticut to be with my brother and baby Owen. The pull of my inner guidance was so strong that despite the fact that it looked a bit like a decision made out of PTSD (which was partially present), I felt I had no choice but to listen to that inner wisdom and also to get crystal clear on my priorities. My husband was supportive, and by the grace of our conservative approach to finances, I was able to resign from my job about six months after Kristen passed.

In 2014, I found myself at a career crossroads. After writing *Vacuum Like No One Is Watching: And Other Lessons from My Mother* in 2011 and taking on some lower-level communications jobs, I was ready to go back out into the world and resume my career path. Life had different plans for me, however.

I had signed on with a new company and had spent two months planning for my new role, but before I was fully on board, they were acquired by another organization. At the time, it was shocking, but as I would later learn, it was a blessing and a sign.

I began sending out resumes again, knowing I had been through much worse but along the way, I pondered why I had been thrown off my career course three times—first after Jack passed, next after Kristen passed, and again when I was ready to resume at a higher level. I had spent a decade trying to work around intense loss. This almost became the last straw for me. I was extremely close to bitter, not better, in those months. I wondered, What was the universe trying to tell me? What was I supposed to do? What *should* I do? How could I be most useful? Was it the same old career I thought I loved but was now eluding me?

At the time, my business partner, Helene, and I were in a social book club together, and we both had an interest in adding spiritual reading to the list of books. We ended up meeting on our own to read, listen, and talk. She shared Wayne Dyer's *I Can See Clearly Now* with me. Dyer's PBS special, his book talk, profoundly affected me. I was mesmerized. My life was again starting to make sense. It wasn't accidental or tragic, but, rather, it was *my path*. In fact, I remember thinking, "Where has this man been my whole life?"

All the other authors Helene shared with me— Eckhart Tolle, Michael A. Singer, Gary Zukav, Esther Hicks, Brené Brown—all authors she had been reading, listening to, and following for many years, also caused me to wonder similarly about them. While I was busy in business, climbing some invisible ladder, grieving intensely, reading books on tragedy across the globe and bereavement, and subsequently falling off that fictitious ladder, I was missing out on something big—really, really big!

I wondered if I could share my newfound wisdom with more people; after all, I was a communication professional. I understood that if indeed I did start a business, if Helene and I made this move in our careers, the core was life coaching. So in 2014, after a decade of pain and love, tragedy and also great kindness, I adapted my career and became a life, success, and spiritual coach.

As we pondered how to craft a business based on spirituality, positive psychology, and philosophy, we considered offering other practitioners rental space for complementary modalities such as yoga, guided meditation, reiki, and a variety of other wellness techniques. We opened the doors of The Center on September 15, 2015. Today, we offer clients one-on-one coaching and group coaching in workshops and seminars, plus collaborate with other practitioners to provide yoga, tai chi, qigong, reiki, sound meditation, guided meditation, and more.

I came to great clarity that coaching was what I was meant to do. Having spent a decade learning how to live my life after tragedy, I realized that perhaps any expertise I had was no longer in the business world. What if I could become, like Wayne Dyer, a teacher of resilience and well-being, spreading the message in my own community? When all conventional models of success start blowing up and life falls apart and back together in unexpected ways, what do you do? I wanted to help others use spirituality, positive psychology, and philosophy to reconnect with themselves, what is real, and who they really are, and to learn how to withstand even the worst occurrence and rebuild a life that is positive, functional, joyful, and purposeful.

During the decade between 2004 and 2014, I lost my nine-year-old son, Jack; nearly lost my marriage (but we made it!); lost a job I loved to a reorganization; lost my little sister, Kristen, to cancer; lost my health for a bit; lost my ability to do my current job; lost another big job opportunity; and lost my understanding of my life and often my sanity. Through all the loss, I gained tremendous clarity—compassion and contentment too—and started to rebuild my career in a direction that suits my soul.

To support clarity in your life, the following chapters will focus on building self-awareness, living with intention, authenticity, alignment, and resilience, and addressing the feeling that something is missing.

Enjoy!

CHAPTER 2

Building Self-Awareness

"Self-awareness is the ability to take an honest look at your life without any attachment to it being right or wrong, good or bad."
—Debbie Ford

Building self-awareness is one of the first steps in coaching. I want you to know yourself. This may seem elementary, but we often operate in a state of unconsciousness, and stress and confusion can develop when we don't take the time to become self-aware. Becoming more conscious of what is really going on in and around us, rather that operating unconsciously on autopilot, can significantly impact our lives.

How many times have you found yourself falling into behaviors out of habit? Some are useful, such as brushing our teeth. Some are not, such as thinking we may not be good enough, overthinking in general, becoming defensive with others, and allowing our ego to overshadow the self. There are many ways in which we do not want to just operate on autopilot. We don't want to live unconsciously our entire lives. We don't want to fall into the trap of automatic behaviors that may keep us stuck.

What is really going on in our lives? Are we paying attention? How would you describe your life today?

What is calling your attention? Have you become weighed down with protective layers from past hurts? Are you ready to soar, having cleared milestones in your life? How do you feel: vibrant and joyful, or weathered and weary? What do you want in life? (This includes leisure as well as family and work.)

Okay, I just pummeled you with questions, but how we feel matters. Paying attention to our own lives is vital! It sounds like the simplest thing in the world, but we tend to avoid paying attention to our own lives because we are afraid we will see something we do not like, or we feel we are not worth our own time and attention. Time and again I hear people say, "I'm so busy, I don't have time to look inside." What they really mean is that they are keeping themselves too busy on purpose, to avoid looking inward, or they feel that spending time with the self is an indulgence they cannot afford. Each and every time I meet clients and work with them to look deeper at themselves and their lives, we find the most amazing people buried under vast quantities of busyness, labels, goals, and expectations!

The Personality Assessment

In addition to all of the previous questions, another tool for creating more self-awareness is a personality assessment. I recommend this for everyone. We are all unique, although our personalities often fall into certain categories. These categories can show us our preferences. Although preferences come from the ego, not the soul, we still operate with these two selves, so it's useful to understand our ego's tendencies. Usually when we read these reports, we are shocked at how accurately they depict our preferences, and feel validated by seeing our likes and dislikes so vividly on paper. In a sense, we feel a little less alone when we read about our personality type, especially if others in our life have not understood some of these tendencies. This information enables us to work with our personalities to create alignment in life, rather than living and working against our natural tendencies.

The Myers-Briggs Type Indicator (MBTI) is a personality assessment tool that allows us to understand our strengths, weaknesses, and preferences. Ultimately, we can use it to align different parts of our life. When we don't honor these preferences and work against our strengths, a high level of confusion or stress can arise; we may feel like failures or loners, or as if we're misunderstood. And as I like to say, the personality assessment's list of weaknesses isn't a big list of things to fix, but rather valuable information we can use to foster understanding.

If you have ever spent time in a job or relationship that is a complete misfit for you, you know that it can grind life to a standstill, draining all of your energy and potentially even making you sick. Understanding and aligning your talents and interests offers an opportunity to create an authentic success you may never have even imagined possible. In this way, the personality assessment can help you flow in the direction of your strengths and experience more success.

Tuning in to Our Emotions

Another way we can build self-awareness is by feeling our emotions, rather than pushing them down or unconsciously acting on them. When we are aware of what we are experiencing and examine it with curiosity, tracing its roots, we can begin to see patterns and use this information to further align and learn about ourselves. Raising your level of consciousness means becoming aware of your thoughts, emotions, and reactions, and allowing them to tell us where we need to heal, grow, or adapt.

While it might seem risky to trust your gut overruling your rational thought process and the safety of familiarity, it is completely sane. We should use our preferences to help us move in the direction that best suits us. When we feel a great deal of resistance, our emotions are trying to give us an indication that we are on the wrong path. We *should* follow our joy.

Now, I know that outside of coaching circles, there is little emphasis on moving toward what you like as a first priority, because of all the "life is hard" messaging we've heard. But what better way to learn more about yourself and align for success than by getting in touch with what you love and what makes you feel alive, and moving toward that?

Conversely, we can also get in touch with ourselves by paying attention to what drains our energy. Who do you enjoy being around? Who do you dislike being around? What are you putting up with? When do you procrastinate? What are you doing that doesn't feel like work, when time goes by fast? The latter is called ecstatic engagement, and is a key to understanding the self.

How do you feel when you're going to work? What do you feel upon waking in the morning? What opportunities exist for you to do more of what you love and less of what you do not love?

Later in this book, in the chapter on contentment, we will look closer at our feelings and finding joy, both of which allow us to honor our true selves.

CHAPTER 3

Living with Intention

"Our intention creates our reality."
—*Dr. Wayne W. Dyer*

I regularly offer a Live by Design (Not Default) workshop in which I facilitate a small group to write their life plans—taking the plan out of their head and putting it down on paper. The elements of the plan include how you would like to be remembered; your priorities; and creating life categories that reflect the people or topics you wish to be investing your time, energy, and resources in, creating a vision for the future, action steps to get there, familiarizing yourself with fears, blocks and limiting beliefs, law of attraction and manifesting, and self care and boundaries. Workshop participants usually realize there are some categories they have deemed important that they are essentially starving of their time and attention. This can bring about tremendous clarity.

We do not have unlimited time and capacity; therefore, prioritization can assist us in determining what to invest in and what we need to say no to. We cannot say yes to everything, as that would leave us feeling drained and dragged-out and living by default—the hallmarks of a "resentful yes," or one that makes us feel as if we're wasting time on pleasing others. Yet many regularly operate on this default setting. Instead, we must learn to say no to the "resentful yes" and spend time on what is meaningful to us.

Setting boundaries and ensuring self-care is another means to create the life of your design rather than a life of reaction. When you are drained and running out of steam, in order to continue to function at optimal levels, you must know what recharges you. This must be something you do for yourself; no one else is responsible for knowing what recharges you. It can be as simple as taking time to read a book, taking a nap or a day off by yourself, a long walk or a visit with a friend, or as elaborate as a day at the spa or a vacation.

Finally, we must keep the bigger picture in mind. Emotionally strong people do not just keep plowing because they see a "Never give up" meme online. Never give up on what? Never give up on *yourself*! Rather than never giving up a specific thing you wanted, never give up on the bigger picture of your own self and dreams. I have seen many people become stuck because they are so attached to one specific job, career, or relationship that is no longer serving them. The key here is growth, and that is achieved by never giving up on you and what you find most meaningful.

Creating a life plan—and getting it out of your head and onto paper—allows you to live with intention. The plan is a guideline to keep you focused and on track with your priorities, ensure that you make time for self, and allowing the space for clear decisions to be made on what *does* and *does not* fit into the plan. The plan also includes creating a vision for the future and identifying action steps that provide clarity to allow you to place your thoughts upon what you want so that you can manifest it. Also, facing our fears, breaking the blocks they create, and rewriting limiting beliefs into empowering beliefs are also steps that enable our life plan to pave the way to living with intention. Lastly, creating a self care routine and healthy boundaries reduces or eliminates resentments and establishes a flow in our lives.

CHAPTER 4

Authenticity

"The authentic self is the soul made visible."
—*Sarah Ban Breathnach*

People pleasing, fitting in, and building self-worth by false measures of success contribute to us living inauthentic lives. Are you trying to be someone else's version of you? Are you living their projection? What is *your* version of you? Are you trying to live up to your younger self's expectation of who you should be? Is it time to update that expectation?

When you find your authenticity and live it, you open the door for others to live authentically. Authenticity is innately attractive to others. On both conscious and subconscious levels, we gravitate toward authentic people. What holds us back from authenticity is the thought that if we were completely authentic, others would not like us. The opposite is true, however. When we are authentic, we become magnets. Living from our true selves resonates with others because other human beings long for authenticity as well.

Think about someone you admire. Are they authentic or are they putting up a false front? I think you will find they are authentic and intensely comfortable with their authenticity.

Our masks are not sustainable. If we continue to hide behind them year after year, we eventually become a caricature of ourselves. Our authenticity makes true connection with other humans possible, and as humans, we are built for connection.

When we are not authentic, we can find ourselves lonely and isolated, using controlling behaviors to protect our mask. When we step into our authenticity, we allow the light of our true selves to shine through for all to see.

CHAPTER 5

Alignment

"I feel glorious dynamic energy. I am active and alive."

—*Louise Hay*

When we are aligned with our authentic selves, we find a flow or ease in life. We line up our actions, behaviors and beliefs with our truest selves to begin attracting what we need and want, and cease attracting what we do not want or what hurts us. It is the equivalent of going downstream rather than upstream. One is easy and the other is hard. When we bravely take off the mask of our false selves, we allow life to flow through us and serve us. We align with this true self, setting ourselves up to find happiness and ultimately feel joy.

I was blessed to have always loved my job. As a communications professional, I was involved in employee and public relations. I was aligned with my skill set as well as my personality, and certainly my authenticity. My interest in other people was sincere and it allowed me to find success and happiness for many years. Until it began to feel like a mask.

I knew it was time to go deeper. After twenty years, half of which I spent learning how to grieve and be resilient, I felt that my true expertise was no longer in communication for the employer to the community or other businesses, but rather communicating principles of positive psychology and spirituality to individuals. I particularly enjoy holding sacred space open for clients to relax, sit back, view their life from a different perspective, gain clarity, learn, and grow in a completely safe and loving environment. Recently, I have been on the road, bringing mindfulness and other coaching lessons into the workplace. I feel a strong sense of alignment with my authentic self. It brings me great joy to connect with individuals and groups, the workplace reminds me of my old work life, and many of my skills are engaged in the same, but more effective, ways.

Does your work suit you? While it may not be your passion, it may serve your life. Does it fit well with your skills? I love hearing bookkeepers talk of the "puzzle" they enjoy solving in finance (especially since the only subject I ever failed was accounting!). I marvel at bridges, knowing that some skilled engineer designed it to support me, my car, and many others as we cross. My friend is a brilliant data analyst, aligned with her skill and interest in detail. She is continually surprised when told how truly talented she is and that not everyone can do what she does. Whether in customer service or back-office administration, sales or human resources, working inside or outside, it is vital to align our work with our preferences. It is important that we appreciate the opportunity to earn a living, but also the opportunity to live while we are at work.

Do you find joy where you are working? Are there people you enjoy working with? Are you challenged in a good way? Are you challenged in a bad way? Do you feel rewarded? Are you able to balance work and life? These are important questions that will help you align your work with your authentic self.

Many of my clients are entrepreneurs. Work-life balance is a common challenge because working solo means they could potentially work 24/7. Work-life balance for them is a discipline. They need to align themselves with the most efficient way of operating and most effective way of caring for family while dropping time wasters such as resistance and diminishing returns from overworking. This is where coaching can make a vast difference.

I have had clients who were ready to quit their jobs because they could not stop it from seeping into every aspect of their lives. Setting boundaries dropping resistance; and learning about ego, the law of attraction, and manifesting can make the difference between feeling misaligned and aligned. After coaching, I have had many of these clients tell me they are more satisfied with their jobs, so they no longer want to leave their job—and they also made more money! Getting clear includes aligning yourself for your own personal success. Interestingly, as a coach I am also self-employed and am now living the same experience as these clients. Personally, I work daily on all the same principles I share with clients and the struggle is real. It does require attention, perseverance, and discipline to create alignment and life balance, but good news is that it can be done, and the rewards are vast! A few of my clients, highly talented and ambitious leaders in business, were striving and never arriving. This means they were doing far more people pleasing than they need to at their level of employment, building resentments, and becoming overwhelmed. This may be a final adjustment after gaining clarity, revisiting our authentic selves, allowing for our own success. Or a client may be speaking to one career goal but resisting it subconsciously. This wastes precious energy and keeps alignment out of reach. This is a form of self sabotage that can be discovered in coaching. Many of my clients seek life balance and in fact, may even think this is a unrealistic goal. Perfectionism, overwork, taking on too many roles, can result in diminishing returns and exhaustion which leads to confusion, so knowing the right level of work for the desired return is critical to living well.

CHAPTER 6

Resilience

"Out of suffering have emerged the strongest souls; the most massive characters are seared with scars."
—*Kahlil Gibran*

Resilience is reframing, refocusing, and rebounding from a setback. It requires creating a path forward while facing a new and challenging reality, and living life despite hardship.

In order to be resilient, over time we begin let go of stories that do not empower us, and move toward a story that does. It does not necessarily mean that anything we experienced should have happened which may be extremely difficult to embrace given the circumstances, or that we deserved it; instead it is an act of acceptance of reality and forward movement. Individuals who feel that acceptance means saying it was all okay or that they wouldn't have it another way may become stuck. Of course there are many things we would change if we could, but accepting what is keeps you moving. It is about allowing a new reality to form, choosing our focus, and determining our reaction and attitude.

If I had had a choice, I would absolutely *not* experience the loss of my son and sister. They would be here with me now. Since I cannot change reality, I must accept our new reality. If I did not, I would be living a life of extreme suffering. I might feel that I do not deserve to be or cannot be happy, or feel like a victim. I realized that any step in that direction would have been self-indulgent at best and martyrdom at worst, and it would hurt all of the people in my life who were already hurting from our family's loss of Jack and Kristen. My ability to accept these losses over time has enabled me to be present for the wonderful people and happenings in my life now. It also allows me to grow by serving others in their memory.

Viktor Frankl, the late psychiatrist and Holocaust survivor, transcended unspeakable atrocities by elevating his state of mind. He wrote, "Everything can be taken from a man but one thing: the last of human freedoms—to choose one's attitude in any given set of circumstances, to choose one's own way." Choosing our way, in a positive way, is exhibiting resilience.

In the face of our suffering, we can stand tall and get clear on our altered path. Despite the challenge, when we become aware of the ego's story that we should stay angry, resentful, or safe by not risking again, we prevent ourselves from being held back. We can and should counter our ego and accept the journey and ap-

preciate that our hardship is ultimately ou[...]
potentially happening for us rather than agai[...]

This shift does not happen quickly; we can[...]
our healing. It requires patience and time. It is [...]
not have all the answers; many hardships offer no ex-
planation of why. Marcus Aurelius said, "The impedi-
ment to action advances action. What stands in the
way becomes the way." The obstacle is the way. Open
up to the perspective that the hardship is happening
for our greater good, for your soul's growth, especially
when it is randomly, painfully, excruciatingly beyond
your control. Transformation and healing are possible
if we are open to accepting our new state.

Frankl was able to transcend his circumstances in
a Nazi concentration camp by envisioning himself
teaching a class on the psychology of what was happening there. This is the ultimate example of the power of the mind.

I take great comfort in a quote from spiritual
teacher and author Eckhart Tolle: "We did not come
here to sleep. We came here to awaken again and
again." Tolle is saying that our lives are a journey toward awakening.

How can you become resilient? How is the re-
framed and refocused reality a life that serves your
highest self? How does the adversity enable you to
grow and serve others? When you see this, you can allow an empowering perspective to open the door to a
life of joy and purpose despite the circumstances.

CHAPTER 7

Something Is Missing

*"If you think there is something missing
in your life it is probably you."*
—*Robert Holden*

I love this quote! Dr. Robert Holden is a wonderful psychologist, Hay House author, and coach. I have had the pleasure of attending his Coach Camp and reading many of his books. He follows up that statement with "More of you is required," and then asks, "What would it look like to add more of you to your life? What would it look like at 10 percent more? Twenty-five percent more? Fifty percent more? A hundred percent more?"

Have you ever felt like something was missing in your life? Perhaps it was during a time of great busyness or after a period of an intense lack of busyness. During these times, take the deep dive. What needs do you have that are not being met? Are you willing to spend time with yourself?

This may be an uncomfortable exercise at first, especially if we have been conditioned to focus on others and have developed negative associations with focusing on ourselves. We may experience exhaustion and resentment if we spend all our energy focusing on others. Resentment is a common by-product of the "I take care of you, and you take care of me" mentality. Make sure you take care of you too! Waiting for others to focus on us in reciprocity is dicey. We may not receive it, and not because someone else doesn't love or appreciate us, but because they may not have the capacity at the moment, or the ability to read our minds, or a whole basket of other reasons.

What else holds us back? We may be scared of what we will find if we connect with ourselves and feel our feelings. But what you will find, if you take the time to look, is your magnificent self. Any feelings you encounter you can and should feel. Becoming comfortable with even the uncomfortable parts of our selves empowers us to operate from our highest self rather than living in shame or suppression. Pushing down our feelings, hiding our inadequacies, feeling that we are in some way less than others, can all lead to a volcanic explosion. Even when this happens, our breakdown can be a breakthrough, knocking down walls, barriers, and falsehoods that keep us low. Honor yourself as you would someone else. You are worthy of your own time—it is required to live a joyful and fulfilled life.

Do include yourself into your own life. Get to know yourself, include activities you enjoy into your routine, pay attention to how you feel and use it as a compass, appreciate your authentic self. When you do, you will find the most amazing person and it will feel so good. I promise.

CHAPTER 8

Compassion

"Love and compassion are necessities, not luxuries.
Without them humanity cannot survive."
—Dalai Lama

Meet everyone, including yourself, with compassion.

Merriam-Webster's Collegiate Dictionary defines compassion as a "Sympathetic consciousness of others' distress together with a desire to alleviate it." In coaching, we speak about empathy for others as feeling as they feel, which activates the desire to alleviate that suffering. We are all energetic beings, sharing and absorbing the energy of others, but some of us are more empathetic than others when presented with the pain and discomfort of others.

British author Karen Armstrong has written numerous books examining religion. In her book *Twelve Steps to a Compassionate Life,* she says, "Compassion is the task of our time." Compassion espouses the Golden Rule, which Armstrong says is the thread

eligions: *Do unto others as you would have
o you.* You would not want anyone to cause
suffering and, therefore, you do not cause
ering for them.

ago, I read Immaculée Ilibagiza's book
Left to Tell, about the Rwandan genocide in the early '90s. Her sentiment has stayed with me all these
years and will forever. When Immaculée was hidden
with seven other women in a bathroom of a pastor's
home—the door covered with an armoire to keep
them from the being found and killed—she thought
of others in the world, particularly the United States,
and prayed that they would not let this atrocity go
unchecked. Surely, she thought, help must be coming. As she waited, crushed against others and eating
very little, she consistently held out hope that people
were coming to help.

Can you imagine that feeling of hiding in fear
and hoping for help? The empathy we feel, imagining
ourselves in that situation is what creates the compassion for action.

Our empathy, however, can sometimes cause us to
look away, for fear of experiencing painful feelings. It
is not easy to become aware of suffering in the world
if we feel helpless. In this case, one might go to the
extreme opposite, which is separation. When we operate from our egos, we define separateness by creating "other" and creating stories about why the other
might deserve what is happening to them.

Jesus taught us to love our enemies. Why is that anything we should do? Why would he advocate such a crazy thing? I'm going to go out on a limb here, but I am not sure we do a very good job as humans at loving our enemies, big and small. Loving our enemies is extremely difficult to do, at least from the ego. From the soul, it's much easier. For example, the late Nelson Mandela chose peace and helped put a stop to the fighting in South Africa, even after twenty-seven years of imprisonment. And Scarlett Lewis, the author of *Nurturing Healing Love: A Mother's Journey of Hope and Forgiveness,* who lost her son Jesse in the Sandy Hook Elementary School shooting, practices and advocates for forgiveness.

Today we live in a world where our exposure to world news is far greater than in previous generations and our fears have much fuel. When we can put the ego into perspective, we can see the divine in everyone, even the most egregious of our own society or in the world, even our enemies. Compassion and love are critical to fulfilling our purpose here, and while it is not easy, it makes the world a kinder place. "Compassion, kindness and forgiveness are good detox agents," Karen Armstrong contends. Why is detoxing necessary? Because our perception of "other" is hurting all of us.

Compassion is appreciation for someone else's journey, opinions, and hardship. It is knowing that we are one. To build our compassion "muscle," we can look at our loved ones, colleagues, acquaintances, and even the strangers around us and ask ourselves, How are we the same? How are we different? What does the difference really matter? Further, we can ask, Can I send them compassion? I hope that more often than not, you say yes.

In order to have compassion for others, we must have compassion for ourselves. Cultivating self-compassion has the ability to change the world, beginning with ourselves. We'll discuss how to develop self-compassion in the next chapter.

CHAPTER 9

Self-Compassion

"You, yourself, as much as anybody in the universe, deserve your love and affection."
—Buddha

Are you able to say to yourself, "I'm doing the best I can at this moment with what I know and have"? We can't have true compassion for others until we find it for ourselves.

Self-judgment and criticism come at a great cost. While many of us were raised to push ourselves hard and not to think too highly of ourselves lest we become arrogant, or for those raised in homes where others were critical of us, we learned the skill of self-judgment. This subtle, or not-so-subtle, negativity toward ourselves can be detrimental. Much self-criticism happens in our own heads, silently labeling us as having done a good enough job or a bad job, and, deeper than that, being good or bad as people. Dumb or smart. Not good enough, not enough, not important.

Negative perceptions of ourselves come from the ego and also from the early education we receive from our families and the world. Today, we see and feel anxiety, depression, and insecurity all around us. We judge ourselves and feel the shame. When we think about these self-judgments, and stop to *hear* them rather than *be* them, we realize that often there is no one we treat as badly as ourselves. This is true even when we do not think we lack self-compassion. A heightened sense of self-judgment can reveal more than you think.

About a year ago for my husband's birthday, I wrote him a little poem about all the things he does well. Some were big, like how Dave is a wonderful father and runs a successful business, and some were small but special, such as his ability to fix everything around the house, including the drain when it is clogged with my hair. Upon my final edits, a thought floated across my mind: "Well, you are pretty worthless!" WOAH! Hello! Where did that come from? Answer: the ego.

It was such a horrible thought, it stopped me in my tracks. In comparison to all the things my husband does well, my ego decided to tell me I was "pretty worthless." In the past, I bet I would only have *felt* that statement rather than *heard* it. It would have been another subconscious feeling that affected my sense of worth and demonstrated a lack of self-compassion. It may have become a subconscious thought that kept me from thinking well of my husband, because thinking well of him might make me feel bad about myself.

This thought required rewiring. I spent some time thinking about what I do well, how I spend my time, who I spend time with and the results of my abilities. I realized that I do many things well including caring for family, sharing my life experience with others, continually reading, studying and learning to best serve my clients, and writing. I also realized a deeper truth. There have been times I have been the heart and conscience for my family. I have sacrificed and focused on what was important, always striving to do the right thing for all concerned. Spending this extra time reconnecting with my gifts and talents was important to combating the negative thought that I was "pretty worthless." Ultimately, I was able to re-establish a sense of worth from that stray destructive thought.

I think we should write a list today of all of the things we do well. Include, like I did for Dave, things big and small. We need to recognize ourselves as people we value. Without compassion for ourselves, we lack true compassion for others, and we will hold them to the same level of abuse we subject ourselves to. We won't want them to shine because we feel dark. When we take time to tune into these thoughts and understand how often we have negative thoughts about ourselves, we can catch the unkindness and judgment, correct the thoughts, and cultivate compassion for ourselves. Our lives will be far better for the love we can show ourselves.

Self-criticism doesn't make you better, but rather creates more insecurity and potentially resentment. In her book *Self-Compassion: The Proven Power of Being Kind to Yourself,* author Kristin Neff, PhD, suggests we nurture ourselves as we would a valued friend. When things go wrong, put the situation into perspective, as if you're considering it for that friend, realizing that we are not always capable of meeting our own expectations or those of others.

Neff's research shows that harsh self-criticism does not result in more success or ambition, but rather causes more insecurity and resentment. Providing yourself with love, acceptance, and security is one of the most important things you can do. Once we do that, we can grow our compassion for others—not just those who are victims—and recognize that everyone is worthy of compassion, even those who have made bad decisions or have hurt others. This shift involves first seeing ourselves as worthy of compassion, which allows for the seeing all of humanity as worthy of compassion as well.

Neff encourages us to recognize any negative perceptions we have of ourselves and our worth as coming from our ego and our conditioning, which we've defined as our upbringing or examples others have provided that show us how the world works. This conditioning, also called domestication by don Miguel Ruiz in his book *The Four Agreements,* is the projection of who we are and how we are expected to behave by our parents, family, society, and those who run institutions such as school or the government. As we grow, we become conditioned to fit into families, society, and our world, and any varying from the "fitting in," as deemed by ourselves and others, can lead to labeling and harsh judgments.

Brené Brown, in her book *The Gifts of Imperfection* and her famous TED Talk, shares the moment her research led to a breakdown she shifted to a spiritual awakening. Her lightbulb moment came when she realized she could not be as compassionate to her children as she thought she was if she was not compassionate to herself. Her research into what she calls wholehearted living demonstrated that the most successful and happy among us (those Abraham Maslow called self-actualized in the 1960s) were compassionate to themselves.

In order to cultivate self-compassion, we need to drop perfectionism. For any perfectionists now reading, that doesn't mean you should drop this book! Perfectionism is often lauded in our society, which makes us feel so very good, but it certainly has its dark side. Many may even feel they are successful because of perfectionism. Although it might be considered a gift, its foundation is fear. Perfectionism, Brown's research shows, is built on the premise of being good enough to protect ourselves from shame and blame.

With perfectionism, the thinking is, "If I'm just good enough, and drive myself hard enough, I will protect myself from any criticism or failure." However, we know that while we can be very effective, there is no true protection from something going wrong (hence the need for resilience). When we do operate out of perfectionist thinking, our reality may be completely shattered when we do still fail. Ultimately, we will experience failure of some kind in our life. Of course, failure gives us a wonderful opportunity to create self-compassion and a broader world view. Pema Chödrön gave a college commencement speech called "Fail, Fail Again, Fail Better," which she later turned it into a book. When we are able to fail and reframe failure into a learning experience, we are practicing self-compassion and also demonstrating our resilience.

Today, affirm for yourself that you are capable. Affirm also that you are doing the best you can. If today is difficult, you may be experiencing what you are meant to experience, to grow in compassion for yourself and others. Treat yourself as you would a wonderful friend. When things go wrong, provide for yourself a soft place to land and be nurtured. I've learned a favorite expression from Helene: "You are exactly where you are meant to be." This simple nine-word sentence speaks volumes for finding compassion for yourself when you are not where your ego thinks you should be!

When we develop the capacity to look at ourselves with kindness and compassion, including even those spots we feel are the most unpleasant parts of ourselves, we are able to grow. When we do not feel like we are growing or we feel stuck, this may be the very rock to look under for healing.

CHAPTER 10

Universal Love
& Oneness

"Every loving thought is true.
Everything else is an appeal for healing
and help regardless of the form it takes."
　　　　　—A Course in Miracles

We are love. We are one. We are all connected. Our job is love.

In this chapter, we will step far, far away from the ego sense of separateness and spend time in the deep connection with universal love and oneness. For the time being, I want you to drop all fear, guilt, sadness, regret, and worry. Discard any discomfort. Sink into a comfortable position. Settle your mind.

Ask yourself, **What is love?**

What comes to mind?

Is it romance? Is it complete comfort? Is it children, God, your pets? Or is it something else entirely?

Now ask, **How does it feel?**

Is it warm, full, round, sweet, endless, bright, all-encompassing? Or does it have some other quality? Write it down.

Over time, many of the teachers of positive psychology, resilience, spirituality, and living well, evolve toward teaching love. It seems that love, as featured in poems, songs, letters, and prayers, is the answer. Since love is an overarching theme, how can we bring more love into our lives? How can we share more love in our lives?

At Hay House Coach Camp 2018, Robert Holden, asked all of us, "How can you be expressing your love more?" After we had spent some time jotting down our answers, he said, "Love is the ultimate coach." Holden even has a mastermind group on love-centered coaching! As he continued to speak of love and its role in coaching, I felt a deep sense of resonance. It was so strong that it made me cry. The feeling of love I have for all of my clients—deep, meaningful, and extremely real—is okay. I am okay to feel that way, and, in fact, he was advising it!

If I felt that way, I was not sure if I was coaching correctly. I doubted myself and wondered why I was so weird. This is how life loves me. (Holden and the late Hay House founder Louise Hay wrote a beautiful book called *Life Loves You.*) It delivers to me messages I need at the right time. I can express love more by continuing what I am doing through coaching and writing, and perhaps even finding new ways to make others feel love. I hope when you read this, you feel love and feel loved.

I would like to share Holden's questions with you and allow you the space to answer.

How could you be expressing your love more?

How does life love you?

Become conscious of the love you are, the love you share, the love you receive. We are capable of thinking above our egos and reaching beyond fear and self-protection. When we can connect to love and to our oneness, we reduces stress, conflict, and tension and live more fully and completely.

CHAPTER 11

Meditation

"The quieter you become, the more you can hear."
—*Ram Dass*

A great two-minute cartoon on mindfulness narrated by Dan Harris, author of *10% Happier* and *Good Morning America* weekend anchor, mentions that a few generations ago, if you said you went running, someone would ask "Who's chasing you? But then doctors and scientists confirmed the benefits of exercise, and we all do it or feel like we should do it. Harris uses this to describe what is happening today with meditation. The science supports it: meditation is the new exercise! It is a beneficial exercise for your brain. You focus on your breath, and if your thoughts wander, you come back and focus on your breath. It really can be that simple.

So many people say to me, "I'm not good at meditating. My mind is too busy." That is the exact point. Our egos are far too busy chattering away. If we take pride in how much we think and how busy we are, we may be extremely reluctant to meditate, as it may seem to be a slowing down of our usefulness. However, the ability to gain control over our thoughts, quieting them bit by bit, has a significant payoff. I use the analogy of a barbell. When you keep lifting the barbell, your arm gets stronger. When you meditate and keep pulling your attention from thoughts to your breath and being in the moment, you are strengthening your ability to come back to your inner guidance from your egoic thoughts.

The power of meditation is even more profound when you realize you can *see* your thoughts rather than *be* your thoughts. Your thinking and your being are separate, and meditation opens the door to feeling this separation. Your thinking has a way of controlling you, and meditation aims to correct the balance, allowing the space for you to hear your inner guidance rather than your ego. Negative thinking causes us tremendous emotional and physical pain. In meditation, you non-judgmentally observe the thinker, further reinforcing that you are not your thoughts. Instead, you are watching your thoughts. You are the one hearing your thoughts. You are not the thought itself.

There are many types of meditation, including mindfulness meditation, breath-awareness meditation, body-scan meditation, and loving-kindness meditation. Mindfulness meditation encourages us to focus on our current surroundings, enabling us to move our minds away from the past or the future and become aware of the present moment, separate from any judgment about it. When I first started coaching, I thought meditation was a form of mindfulness, but actually the opposite is true. Mindfulness, which I will talk about in an upcoming chapter, is a living meditation.

A body-scan meditation focuses on parts of the body and noticing and releasing any tension. Visualization is a useful part of this meditation.

Loving-kindness meditation, also known as metta meditation, cultivates love and kindness toward everything and is aimed at reducing stress and sending loving kindness into the world. When we are significantly challenged by a particular person, we can use a loving kindness meditation to practice the act of extending happiness, peace, and wellness to others. It is easiest to start with someone you think kindly of, then move to a neutral figure in your life, and then ultimately to the person you are finding most frustrating. Meditation is a secular way of centering ourselves, and the science supporting its usefulness in our modern lives mounts. In many guided meditation practices, you bring compassion to yourself and others, a practice that also reduces stress and contentiousness. It is as easy as starting with just a minute a day and working up to ten minutes twice a day. There are many guided meditations on the Internet and You-Tube, which can be found simply by searching for "guided meditation." Meditation apps such as Calm, Breathe, Headspace, and Dan Harris's 10% Happier:

Meditation, to name a few, offer us the opportunity for guided meditation of a variety of lengths of time, at any time. You may see change in as little as a month.

Previously, we spoke about ego, and it keeps coming up again and again; it is that foundational in coaching. You may even find it annoying that I keep mentioning it. If that's the case, know that it's the ego that is annoyed! While the ego itself is not arrogance or boastfulness, it is your center of self-importance and it likes to run the show. It is a part of our mind that keeps us busy by focusing on problems, and in its own way keeps us safe by making stories that create a sense of understanding of the world. There is growing evidence today that people are suffering from anxiety and stress, and the ego has a great deal to do with it. In meditation, we tame the ego by creating stillness, and through this stillness we begin to hear our inner guidance.

I started meditating for the first time when we were training as coaches and creating a business plan. I used to keep a notebook next to me because after meditation, I would be flooded with ideas for business. Some of the ideas even felt like they were coming from my core and not my brain, such as the name Center for Clarity, Compassion, and Contentment and my vision for the logo. In meditation the goal is to let thoughts arise and float by, and return to our breath and "get into the gap." By doing so, we free up mental space that allows us to reduce stress and come to clarity on important topics.

CHAPTER 12

Fear versus Love

"Live life as if everything is rigged in your favor."
—Rumi

In all the great spiritual traditions there is a concept of fear versus love. You are either in *fear,* which is an overarching category for worry, doubt, guilt, suspicion, or anxiety, or you are in **love,** which is an overarching category of oneness, faith, trust, abundance, and spirituality. The theory is that we cannot be in both fear and love at the same time. Therefore, if we are in fear, we are not in love—and, of course, I do not mean romantic love.

When we understand these two opposing forces, we can actively move ourselves from fear when we recognize it. We can have fearful thoughts and compassionately begin creating counter-thoughts to move toward a more loving state of mind. For example, when you worry about work, you can recognize that it is just a worry, not a fact. Whatever you are concerned about is a projection of the future, a mental construct that attempts to anticipate the problem ahead. If you were to counter those fearful thoughts with "I am sure I can handle whatever happens, as there have been many challenges in the past that I have navigated successfully," you would be moving into a more loving place. Even if you hadn't been able to navigate past challenges successfully, you could still move to a loving thought: "I am sure all will be well and I will be supported."

We can always choose to believe the best, no matter our prior experience. However, based on our prior experience, we will know how difficult it is to retrain the brain to see the best. Countering negative thoughts with a more loving response is a tool to improve the quality of your life and also the lives of others around you.

In some instances, we may be perceiving what is happening today through the lens of previous traumas, which elevates our level of fear. Trauma-informed care is based on understanding that previous traumas cause us to develop coping mechanisms and perceptions that persist even after the trauma has ceased. Perceptions and coping abilities based on crisis, chaos, or trauma and may interfere with our ability to perceive or cope with our current situation in a healthy way.

Understanding that previous traumas may inform behavior, even if we have not experienced something similar, is important to our ability to extend compassion to others, who may behave in ways that are confusing to us. Even when we are not traumatized but have been stressed or have experienced a period of chaos, we may operate in crisis mode for an extended time and become triggered by situations that are similar. The ego moves front and center in traumatic or prolonged stressful situations to protect our experience of life.

While writing this book, I had to do a fear-versus-love exercise many times over. In the beginning, it was fear that I couldn't write; later it was fear that what I wrote wasn't any good. Even later I was hit with a lightning bolt of thought: "How am I going to get the formatting, cover, ISBN number, and editing all done by my deadline?!" After enjoying about an hour of sheer joy from finishing the text, a sense of darkness washed over me.

My ego took off running. "How long will the next steps take? How complicated will they be? Wait a minute—the bigger problem is whether or not I've written anything good! Is it even good enough for all that effort? Perhaps it's not good and this was all a waste of time. I bet I wrote what everyone knows already." And on and on! I needed to interrupt that intense fear with love.

I stopped. I meditated. I created a new thought that all the next steps would be put on a list I would deal with in the morning. I created another new thought that I am sure if my work is meant to be seen,

I will be able to navigate this challenge. I moved from fear to love in my thoughts and continue to do so. I had to calm myself down, as we often need to do, and should be empowered to do regularly.

Try using fear versus love as an exercise in your life. Is there something causing you fear now? The next fearful thought you have, meet it with a loving and supportive response.

CHAPTER 13

Scarcity versus Abundance

"Like the air you breathe, abundance in all things is available to you. Your life will simply be as good as you allow it to be."
—Abraham Hicks

A scarcity mind-set focuses on "not enough." Fear that there is not enough to go around makes us fear that we will lose out. Thoughts such as "I don't have enough," "There isn't enough," "I am not enough," "I am feeling a lack," or "I am lacking" alter our perception of the world around us.

Abundance, on the other hand, is having plenty of what you need. An abundance mind-set is feeling that you have enough and will have enough. A shift to an abundance mind-set from a scarcity mind-set can be the difference between well-being and happiness or victimhood and misery. Believing there is enough and you are enough is the most compassionate tool you possess, and it enables you to have compassion for others. When we fear scarcity, we are not willing to share or extend ourselves because we feel our needs are not being met or may not be met for ourselves and our family. In her book *The Soul of Money,* Lynne Twist tells us that in order to break the myth of scarcity, we need to live in a mind-set of sufficiency. "What we appreciate, appreciates. . . . When you share it, it gets bigger."

How can we possibly have a mind-set of sufficiency with all the advertising around us? It's a major contributor to a feeling of lack in our society. Every television or Internet commercial is encouraging you to believe that if you just had their product, you would be better. We are bombarded daily with the message that we need more and that we do not have enough! These messages reinforce that we need more and more even if we can't afford it.

To take a common example, in the past few years there has been a significant increase in the concern about whether or not we have enough money for retirement. "Will I have enough money later to do what I would like to do?" is a question weighing heavily on many minds. People with good pensions talk lovingly about them, and understandably so, as pensions have largely gone away. Today there is more of an emphasis on personal investment. Whether we have enough or not is subjective, and it can lead us to anxiety about the future, feeling less than or not enough, as if we don't have enough, or as if we haven't picked the right career. It may lead to any number of thoughts, not the least of which is "I don't want to be a desolate old person in a nursing home with nothing!"

Okay, if you're worried, let's recap. You are doing the best you can. If you aren't doing the best you can, do the best you can starting now. Calm yourself, and take action knowing that you will be supported. Here is an example. If you are in sales and you haven't been the most diligent in following your sales model resulting in less them stellar deal closings, you would decide to follow the sales model next year to gain better results. Parenting offers us another vivid example. You have lost your temper with your child and find yourself yelling and feeling out of control. Rather than feeling awful, creating imaginary stories about how you have damaged your child, refocus on some key values and know that the next minute, hour, and days offer an opportunity to perform better, calmer and more in line with your values. Again, wellness involves using your imagination for your good, not your detriment. So when we fail, and we use the failure to predict our future failures without taking into consideration our ability to choose, we are using our imagination to our detriment. When we fail, use the failure as a lesson and a reinforcement of what we do not want and visualize a better future, we are using our imagination for our good.

Anyone who can balance scarcity versus abundance can enjoy today as well as tomorrow. After all, your life is happening now, and while planning for tomorrow is absolutely a worthy endeavor, and having no plan is not advisable, we need to shift our worry into action, then believe in good results. Our worry alone does not produce benefits, yet it causes much stress.

I had my own reality check on this a few years ago when we opened. Helene and I were talking about business, and I mentioned that my mother had said "Do I wish you had a six-figure job with retirement benefits? Yes, but I like your determination!" I had laughed when Mom said that, and asked, "Do you think I don't have a retirement plan? I have been working for twenty years and have always contributed to a 401(k), and Dave and I have invested for twenty years in a joint account too." This really got me thinking: "Am I doing the wrong thing for my family by going into business for myself? Will there be enough?"

As I shared my self-doubt, Helene laughed. She said, "You have worked for the past twenty years. I have been a stay-at-home mother for the past seventeen." What a reality check. Was Helene worried? No. Was I worried because someone I love shared her worry about me with me? Yes. Now, my mother always has my best interest in mind, and we are extremely close. I think she is amazing, and I wrote my first book, *Vacuum Like No One Is Watching: And Other Lessons from My Mother,* about her! I could not have picked a better mom to be born to. She truly is the queen of positivity, which was the premise of the book. Her statement about my finances was based on my best interest, and that is what makes it such a good example. This particular worry, about her child's well-being, was totally normal.

Keeping this in mind, we need to be conscious of when a worry is ours and when it belongs to others, and not get them confused. We can become aware of self-doubt and the ways external messages worm their way into our minds.

How do you perceive the future? Is it grim or bright? Which is true? Realizing the fiction of our future, something in my last book I called ficture, can enable us to see clearly and compassionately. Managing our perception and understanding how this is creating our reality is life changing. Have you ever heard the story about tourists walking by a resident and asking, "What is it like here?" I will summarize in my own words, as I have heard many tell this story....

The tourists ask, "Is this a good place to live?" In return, the man says, "Well, what is it like where you live now?" They respond, "Oh, it's not pleasant. It's edgy, frustrating, harsh." So the man says, "It's like that here too."

Later, other people walk by and ask the same question, and the man counters with his own same question. This time, the tourists reply, "Oh, it is nice and people are friendly." The man says, "It's like that here too."

The point of this story is that we see what we are looking for and what we believe. Although there are clearly some neighborhoods more hostile than others, in general, however all things being equal, we can see that some people even in our own communities see a scary world and others see a beautiful world. If you are wondering where you fall and you feel like you are somewhere in the middle—aware of dangers in the world, but generally open and happy and loving and certainly not hostile—I offer this extension: beware of seeing too much hostility, lest you become hostile, and look for friendly if you want to live in friendliness and stay friendly. Our minds are powerful! They can manifest what we are feeling and thinking.

If we live in a scarcity mind-set, we will feel lack all around us. If we live in an abundant mind-set, we will see and feel evidence that we are well supported. As you make your own mind a great place to live, you will open up new capacities to extend love to your precious self and others in the world we share.

CHAPTER 14

Spirituality

"Spirituality is a brave search for the truth about existence, fearlessly peering into the mysterious nature of life."
—Elizabeth Lesser

The term "spiritual but not religious" (SBNR) is becoming common. More and more people seek to connect to spirituality separate from traditional religion and its institutions. Life coaching is a field based on positive psychology, and much of positive psychology takes the best and most common parts from religious traditions.

There are many spiritual leaders we admire, and more that we may not even be aware of whose teachings can deeply and profoundly affect our lives. Learning Lao-tzu's teachings in the Tao Te Ching has changed my life and had a positive impact on my coaching. I only found the wonderful tradition of Taoism through the book *Change Your Thoughts—*

Change Your Life: Living the Wisdom of the Tao by Dr. Wayne Dyer. I have used this book for a facilitated book club at The Center for the past three years, and after several readings of the book and several times through the four-week book club, it has completely tuned me into life's unfolding. Life has its own path and purpose, that may or may not make sense to me. This has offered me profound peace. I was raised a Catholic, and I'm raising my own family as Lutherans, and I have found that my exploration of *all* traditions has become one of my greatest joys. "Jesus, Lao-tzu, Buddha, Krishna, and Yogananda walk into a bar...." I just love them all!

The authors who help deepen my understanding include Marianne Williamson, Gabrielle Bernstein, Pema Chödrön, Eckhart Tolle, Michael Singer, Karen Armstrong, and many others, such as my hero, the late Wayne Dyer. Our Center is inspired by all of them and the desire to bring their work and wisdom to others in a "main street" fashion through coaching, workshops, seminars, and programs that are fun and engaging. This has become part of my life's purpose, and it's still evolving for me as I grow through study, coaching, training, and living. As we live and study the principles of positive psychology and spirituality, I find myself encouraging clients to step away from society's messaging, which often gets in the way of living well. This is as common a theme as the ego! In the Contentment chapter, we will explore this in greater depth.

In all of these teachers' works, the most beautiful concept reinforced for me is that we are magnificent spiritual beings having a human experience, and are here to grow and learn and awaken throughout our time. You and I came from well-being and love, and to well-being and love we must strive to ensure, maintain, or return. Our coaching practice is Inspired Life Coaching. We work to stay connected through study, meditation, and faith to serve our clients to the best of our abilities, and to facilitate the return to well-being.

At our center, all traditions are welcome. We use words such as "God," "Universe," and "Source"; these refer to a power greater than us, a creator. (Over the years, I've found that I like to use the word "Universe," but I am open to any expression of a higher power.) When we were preparing to open the Center, a friend mentioned to me that she noticed something I had posted online, a picture of some journals that used the word "God," and didn't think I could or should do that. I did what I often do: defended my actions and noted I was at a church expo, so it was okay, but I left feeling a little stirred up. On the drive home I realized that I can talk about God all I want. I am self-employed. I am not excluding anyone based on their beliefs. In fact, spiritual coaching is on the rise because people desire *more* connection, and both Helene and I claim "spiritual coach" as part of our title.

On the drive home that day in 2015, I realized that my friend's comment was from a very well-intentioned place, and was a reflection of her own fear and good opinion. It brought to mind Wayne Dyer's frequent recounting of Abraham Maslow's advice that to be a self-actualized person, "it is important to be independent of the good opinion of others." While driving, I declared out loud, "God is in the building!" My new business was inspired by a higher power, and any success would be realized by the higher power. In the past four years as a coach, it has not only benefited my clients and groups, but my own life—tremendously!

Each fall and spring, I enjoy going to the library book sale and finding religious texts and more books by these special authors. I then share them, through honor system in our own library at the Center and by giving them away, with anyone who walks in our doors.

You do not even want to see my "to read" list. It is vast!

As we grow in life, may we also glow. The more you move ego to the side and let your soul appear, the easier it is to accept a higher power and all that it has provided and will provide in our lives.

CHAPTER 15

Contentment

"Contentment is the only real wealth."
—Alfred Nobel

On to our third pillar. When clarity and compassion are incorporated in your life, contentment is possible.

In our corner of the world where most people have food, shelter, safety, and clean water, how is it possible for us to be so discontented? From my corner, I see so many suffering from overscheduling, overcomplexity, overspending, and overburdening ourselves with "should." This is legitimate suffering that occurs because we are measuring ourselves by false standards. For anyone who has ever read a Facebook post and felt less than, you know what I mean. Anyone who has been triggered by a loved one's promotion when you are feeling low, or sheepish that you live in a small house while others live in huge homes in your same neighborhood, you know too.

I am also human. I have compared myself unfavorably to others and felt bad. I have even compared myself with Helene. Think about the natural tendency for us as business partners to feel like the other is perhaps supporting the business more, serving more clients, a better coach. The temptation to compare is a real threat. What part of me might fall victim to this? Yes, you guessed it: EGO.

How are we measuring our worth, achievement, and expectation of a life well lived? What is successful living to you? What is authentic success to you? Are you unfavorably comparing yourself to others? We must recognize that comparison is one of the greatest joy stealers.

In what ways has our ego created stories that we lack time, ability, money, or energy (the scarcity mind-set discussed earlier), and how do we react? In what ways can we counter that story? Even if there is a lack that needs to be filled, for the moment we can focus on what is plentiful as a tool for contentment.

Beware that the ego wants to keep you focused on lack and not reconnecting with what is present that you can appreciate, because the ego is a problem solver. Our egos will spend all day and all night on what is wrong if we let them, as I am sure you have already noticed now that you have become aware that it is part of your mind and not who you are. The key here is, you don't need to let it do all that overtime! Know when to tell the ego to call it a day, punch out, take a long lunch break—whatever you need to do to re-claim your peace.

There is not a chapter in this book in which the ego does not play a part. You can interrupt the ego's rampage by simply countering the negative thoughts and problems with thoughts of how blessed you are, and you will begin to feel the lightening of your spirit. Examine the ways in which you are looking for something outside of yourself to bring you internal happiness. When we are feeling stuck, we need to reframe the story. As the novelist Rita Mae Brown wrote, "Insanity is doing the same thing over and over again, but expecting different results." When we are stuck, we should modify our behaviors, examine our thoughts, note negative thoughts, and counter them. Then we can make new plans or changes that will move us out of stagnation and back into flow.

CHAPTER 16

Gratitude

"Be an appreciator, not a depreciator."
—Dr. Wayne Dyer

In my group programs, I describe that "good" is an expectation, and because of this, we put all that is good in our life on a figurative shelf, where it grows dusty, while we allow our attention to go to our problems. This is the specialty work of ego, which is always looking to be the problem solver. Your ego might even go as far as to tell you that you cannot be happy until all is fixed.

The intentional act of spending time and mental energy on everything that we are grateful for is incredibly *powerful*! I liken it to pulling all the good in your life off the shelf and appreciating each item, dusting them all off, feeling those joys, reconnecting with all that is good, and letting it multiply. This simple act sets us free from chronic discontent. But it is a practice, and it works very well while we are doing it and not so well when we don't. When we aren't feeling so well, the last thing we think to do is sit in gratitude. It is so hard to remember that we can use this practice to help get ourselves into a better mental place. It is the last thing we think of—and the first thing we should do!

In one of the most beautiful meditation videos on YouTube, David Steindl-Rast's "A Good Day" (you-tube.com/watch?v=3Zl9puhwiyw), we can melt into the gift of our lives by listening to his words. This five-and-a-half-minute video set to beautiful music and magnificent images brings us back to the awakening of the day, to the blessing of clean water, to the joy of people in our lives. He challenges us to cultivate a response to each unique day as if it were the first and last day of our lives. Our eyes open to meet the world, we see the formation of clouds in the sky and the faces of people we meet, with a story behind their faces that resembles that all of their ancestors. We open our heart to the blessings of today.

Grab a journal and start noting your "gratefuls" today. Each day, write down at least three points of gratitude. I recently just started morning and evening gratitude, in which I write at least three at each time of day. One of my favorite points, especially for my morning gratitude practice, is "I am grateful for my bed, pillow, blankets." I loved finding out that the late Louise Hay, author, coach, and creator of the amazing publishing company Hay House, used to thank her bed every day. I thoroughly appreciate a good night's rest and the comfort that I am blessed to have in my life. I think of others who are sleeping on pallets and on hay in other parts of the world, and try never to take this level of creature comfort for granted.

Heat. I appreciate that too, especially living in Upstate New York. I am thankful for my home, heat, clean water, my bed, and a good night's rest, in addition to the more obvious "gratefuls," such as my wonderful son Steven (now twenty-two!) and my nephew Owen (now ten!), my parents and step-parents, and, of course, my husband, Dave; my many family members and friends; my business partner, Helene—the list can go on for days.

Despite the hurt and loss, even in the depths of despair, I was afforded some comforts to ease my suffering. Blessed was I to even have images in my head immediately after losing Jack of mothers with hurt children crying for help on the roadside in war-torn areas; they helped me reconnect with my strength. We were helped out of our car accident, transported to a hospital, cared for to the best of everyone's ability, and safe until our ultimate lowest moment of realizing we would lose Jack. We were helped. We were helped by many after that day. We are helped by Jack to this day. I feel his presence more than ever now, fourteen years later. My understanding of how we transition in death and that there is no real death allows me to find comfort and peace. My belief in something bigger than me enables me to live and to *own* this path in life without a sense bitterness. "I suspend my need to know *why* for the day I die," is my mantra. I have come to know that living separated from Jack is part of my life's path, and perhaps teaching others how to develop resilience by transcending their circumstances is my purpose. I talk to many bereaved parents and share my story with them to give them hope that they can function and go on to live full lives for their loved ones. In the beginning of this lifelong journey, it does not seem possible. Others who walked this path before me shared that message with me.

I am grateful for having Jack here with me for nine years, and would not trade him in exchange for relief from the pain.

When I give speeches, I mention that when you have a beloved person in your life—or even if it's you—who is experiencing the perfect storm of events, so much that you can't even believe it, I want to talk to that person, even if it is just for coffee. I want someone in that much pain to know all that I have been sharing in this book. Not just my personal story, but, much more, the story of life. The real story of life, our life's purpose, and the hope that lies ahead. When all our picket fences are broken and burned, we have all we need inside us to continue on. It requires taking one step at a time, bit by bit, in little PacMan bites, as my grief counselor used to say.

When we do, we are appreciating what is before us, while we honor what has left us. For many years now I have said, "All forward movement counts!"

CHAPTER 17

Stress Consciousness

*"The greatest weapon against stress
is our ability to choose one thought over another."*
—William James

What stresses you? Stress consciousness is getting in touch with your stressors and determining what is in your control and what is out of your control. In my "Transform Your Stress" seminar, I teach that although we want things to be a certain way, we may need to allow them to be as they are.

One of my favorite concepts is Eckhart Tolle's summary of stress: "We suffer when we do not accept the 'is-ness' of things." I also like his other beautiful statement, "Stress is being here and wanting to be there." When we don't accept this is-ness, we suffer from wanting things to be another way.

Our suffering is stress. We can take action to change things we don't like, which is a healthy approach to moving toward change. But when we cannot change something, we need to release the expectation. As we become conscious of what is stressing us, we can determine what we need to change and what we need to accept. Of course, our egos are at play here too. What is "supposed" to happen or how things "should be" is the work of ego, not soul. It is our false self trying to categorize right, wrong, good, bad, better, worse, fair, unfair, appropriate, inappropriate, too much, not enough. When we understand what is happening, we can view it all as simply thoughts and examine the usefulness of those thoughts. Do they empower, or have they disempowered us?

Our perceptions are driving our stress. When we perceive threat, we are more stressed. When we perceive smooth sailing, we are not stressed. It is not just as simple as we are threatened or we are not; we can also feel more stressed when we think nonstop about a stressful situation. This completely drains our energy and increases our stress.

A major concern today is how stressed our population is becoming by political disagreements. The discussion has gotten so contentious that it is often uncivil. Why? Because individuals may feel the stakes are so high. I credit Lao-tzu with helping me keep a balanced demeanor within this political environment. His perspective of life unfolding whether we like it or not, has become a stabilizing belief for me and one that I share with others. We do not know the big picture, nor are we in charge of life's unfolding.

In ways we may not understand, any negative circumstance may be causing a necessary change and domino of events. In this way, we can look at situations that make us feel out of control and remember that we aren't in control. Life is taking its path. We can respond to it, but we are certainly not in control of it.

We may feel stressed by discussions happening around us at work or among family members. One of the quickest ways to release the stress is to let go of the need to argue, debate, or fix the situation. Return to a state of openness to another's opinion, understanding that, in fact, you do not need to change it. It is not an either-or proposition; we can live in a world where multiple opinions exist. Remember it is the ego that has little tolerance. It is the ego that wants to be right. It is the ego that needs to fix the other person's understanding. It is the ego that feels hurt if it feels attacked by what the other person is saying. Challenge yourself to explore the ways in which you become impassioned (or pissed!) at the comments. Ask yourself: What part of the discussion offended you? What part of you is offended? It is not the all of you. It is part of you. It is your ego.

Your soul knows that what Lao-tzu shared 2,500 years ago is true: the world is unfolding as it should, whether we like it or not. Whatever your political opinions, you may be surprised to learn that 1) you are not controlling the world, and 2) you are probably not aware (unless you are psychic) of all the ways what is happening now creates a ripple effect, causing a number of changes, potentially even and especially the kind of change you would like to see. For instance, if you believe strongly in climate change and you are upset about any elimination of programs that address this particular problem, you can believe that this is happening to cause more people to pay attention and get active. It may ultimately result in the very thing you would like to see. This is the ripple effect of life's unfolding.

Let's take a milder example than politics. Let's say you are stuck in traffic and completely frustrated that you are not getting where you need to be. Odds are that life will not only go on, but you may never know the full meaning of being delayed. What if being farther down the road at a certain time meant colliding with another car when it slipped on ice? This is just a fictitious scenario, but what if? Trusting that you are exactly where you are meant to be is the less stressful thing to do. Try it as often as you can as an exercise in patience, creating calm, and reducing the stress you feel in your body.

The flexible reed bends, while the brittle branch breaks. This paraphrasing of timeless wisdom from Lao-tzu is being demonstrated daily in our world. When we feel out of control, we tend to become more controlling to minimizing risk. In recent times, we have seen increases as well as decreases in the degree of tolerance of racial conflicts. When it increases, the brittle, rigid branch is certainly being tested. When we are able to demonstrate flexibility and understanding, to become open to what we do not fully understand and the ways in which life is unfolding, we are able to flow with life rather than feeling like it is for us or against us.

CHAPTER 18

Feelings Are Meant to Be Felt

*"We cannot selectively numb emotions,
when we numb the painful emotions,
we also numb the positive ones."*
—Brené Brown

I touched briefly on the idea of experiencing our emotions in "Building Self-Awareness" and again in "Stress Consciousness." Feeling our feelings, honoring them, and becoming more open to exploring them can allow us to find more self-compassion and contentment. Rather than pushing everything down, we can take stock of how we are feeling and what is commonly coming up for us, and use our feelings to check in with ourselves. Over time, brushing off or stuffing down our true feelings can end in a volcanic explosion. Make a vow to no longer operate on a business-as-usual model, pushing forward always and pushing aside your feelings.

There is a misconception that our feelings make us weak, but, in fact, the opposite is true. Our feelings can show us how alive we are and keep us connected to empathy. There is strength in the clearing of emotions on a regular basis. We can learn more about our triggers and why we feel certain ways, and use this to create greater self-awareness. Start with: What is coming up for you today?

Gabrielle Bernstein has a tool for dealing with our emotions, and recognizing that fear plays a significant role. In her *Fear Inventory,* she asks us to describe our fear today (aka worry for today) and determine how we would act if fear (worry) was not a factor.

A Course in Miracles shares, "Nothing you understand is fearful. It is only the hidden that can terrify, not for what it is, but for its hidden-ness." When we bring any of our feelings to the light, we can defuse the fearful charge and increase our opportunity for joy.

When you are experiencing exceptionally good emotions, take note. In those cases, we need to spend a little more time with them. According to Rick Hanson, PhD, who shares the vivid expression that we are "Teflon for good and Velcro for bad," our brains don't naturally stay with happy emotions for long but ruminate on bad ones for a much longer. In order to retrain your brain, you can purposefully take the good feeling and stay with it, not allowing yourself to immediately move to the next thing. Bask in the good feeling for at least five minutes.

This trains your brain to recognize and feel more of these positive feelings.

Recently, I saw a news segment about ice cream sprinkles and how much joy they create for children and adults alike. The joy you see and feel when you have an ice cream cone with sprinkles can be completely lost if you think it is too silly to feel. If you are so absorbed in other feelings and thoughts that you deny joyful feelings when they come your way, you are missing out. I told the sprinkles story to someone and they said "I don't like sprinkles." I said, "How about hard chocolate coating?" "Yes!" she said joyfully. " Me too!" I replied. "How does it make you feel? I know for me, it reminds me of having an afternoon free and going to the dairy circus when I was a teen." She too, recalled a memory that made her feel joyful.

Joy is mostly found in small things, and by allowing ourselves to perceive and feel small moments of fun, we are truly honoring our highest selves. That stressed-out, super serious self is not who we really are, but the feeling we get when we let the worries of yesterday and tomorrow and all of the world's chaos and stress pile on top of us is very real. Make friends with all your feelings and allow them to speak to you. Our feelings are meant to be felt, and connecting with them in a more thoughtful way can ease our suffering and increase our joy.

CHAPTER 19

Your Life as Story

"The privilege of a lifetime is being who you are."
—Joseph Campbell

You are the hero of your own life story. Joseph Campbell, the late American mythologist, determined that there was a common story line in all myths across all cultures. He called this the hero's journey, and it involves: The Call to action, Crossing the threshold, Appearance of helpers and guardians, Challenges and temptations, the Abyss: transformation of the old in revelation, Atonement and The return home. Screenwriters and novelists use this as a template to create their movies and novels. A return home in the movies is a return to the place the hero came from, but for us it could be called a return home to our higher selves.

When looked at through a psychological lens, we see the symbolism in our stories. As the hero in our own life, we experience a call to action when we are challenged and change needs to be made. We are met with helpers and guardians too. Have you ever felt that a certain person in your life arrived to impart a special wisdom necessary for that time? I certainly have. Our helpers come in many forms and not everyone stays in our lives forever. They may be with us for a season or a reason in the bigger picture of our lives.

Challenges and temptations lead you, the hero, to the "abyss" where there is a moment (or moments) of transformation. The death of your old self and the birth of your new self occurs, and you continue on the path of atonement or reckoning. You return home with gifts, specifically the new knowledge you have about your life's purpose in relation to the challenge.

If you've ever seen the movie *Garden State,* written, directed, and starring Zach Braff, you may remember the scene where he builds into the story a literal abyss, a potentially infinite hole in the ground that he overlays on the figurative abyss of his character's journey. The characters can be seen standing on the edge in the pouring rain, screaming into this infinite abyss. This is his turning point, his moment of transformation as he continues on to reckoning in a conversation with his father, and his return home with greater knowledge and purpose. Braff's character has transformed along his personal hero's journey.

How does it feel to be the hero of your own life story? Are you able to see your journey from this perspective? Are you able to see the helpers and guardians, the transformations in your life?

Joseph Campbell believed that the privilege of a lifetime is to be ourselves, and that we should honor our lives by following our joy. "Follow your bliss" is his famous quote about how we should honor our lives. When we do so, Campbell—and many coaches, authors, and spiritual teachers—believes that we find our purpose.

What is your hero's journey? Are you able to view your life from this viewpoint and feel empowered by the path that has been laid behind you, and open to the path that stretches out before you? Even if you have experienced change reluctantly at times, can you see that it was yours for a purpose? This perspective can help us avoid victimhood. Many have experienced tragedy, pain, and suffering, and our acceptance of our path as part of who we are eases our suffering and allows us to step into our own power and purpose. Our challenges, triumphs, and tragedies serve our highest self and bring us closer to home.

Campbell's work resonates deeply with me, as I do feel like I live a far deeper and richer life for having taken my own hero's journey. The way I see it, *all roads* lead me home.

CHAPTER 20

Happiness

"There is no way to happiness, happiness is the way. "
—Thich Nhat Hanh

Happiness is triggered by external elements that we allow to make us happy. Joy (to be discussed in the last chapter) is far greater. We must desire to be happy to respond to situations with a feeling of happiness. The ego can lead us to believe that if certain conditions are met, we can be happy, and if not, we cannot be happy. In reality, happiness is available to us now, all the time and any time, if we allow it into our lives. This moment is your life. Happiness occurs when you open your eyes to it.

Robert Holden, PhD, started his Happiness Project in 1994, as part of a government-sponsored study. His research indicated that while we have more of everything, we aren't actually happier. His eight-week course on happiness became a huge success. He claims the biggest cause of unhappiness is forgetting who we are and that our true nature is joy. What inhibits our true nature and keeps us from happiness? Being too consumed with guilt, fear, doubt, worry, martyrdom, limiting belief that we can't be too happy or it's not good. These feelings can be so intense and all-consuming that we miss moments that would bring us happiness. The antidote: move fears out of the way and get in touch with who you are, what you love, and what really inspires you. Also, look for happiness everywhere.

If you have been feeling unhappy or wish to cultivate a greater sense of happiness, simply allow yourself to be happier. Look for happy scenes around you. To reconnect with the happiness that already exists, you cross a bridge psychologically and spiritually. This is the bridge that bypasses the ego, allowing you to reconnect with your happiness. Your happiness can be boundless if you are willing to drop the fear your ego is feeding you about not having time, resources, or the worth to be happy. It flourishes when we rewrite limiting beliefs that require us to earn our happiness. It pops up for us when we let go of conditional happiness and look around us for everyday goodness in our lives. Happiness can be found in a good book, a cup of tea, a sunny day, our favorite show, a great aroma or meal, and, of course, loving people around us. When we stop to savor it, we have found it.

Many years ago when I was a teenager, my mother, father, sister Kristen, and I were all waiting to view our Olan Mills portraits. This was back in the day when you went twice: first to take the photos, then to view them. There was a huge backlog for some reason, perhaps disgruntled customers, and our wait was hours long. We started out irritated but ended up happy; we were laughing, joking, and telling stories, and almost forgot where we were. We were together, and we became lost in our own happiness.

In the movie *Jerry Maguire,* the lead character gives us a beautiful view of being happy in the scene where he is looking for a song to sing along to in his car. He lands on "Free Fallin'" by Tom Petty. As he belts out the lyrics he knows, and some he doesn't, he is expressing his extreme happiness. Whenever I have extreme moments of happiness like that, I like to sing out loud too!

The present moment offers so many opportunities for happiness, hidden by our deep thought and rumination about the past and the future. When we spend mental time in the past and future, we are not in the now. Eckhart Tolle's book *The Power of Now* centers on the concept that the present moment, the now, is all that exists. The past is gone and the future hasn't happened yet. He reinforces that when we are in the present moment, we can connect to happiness by appreciating the moment without the burden of past and future.

Even when it comes to arguments or disagreements with others, we must ask ourselves whether we want to be right or happy. Being right may be factual, but it may also be divisive or accelerate an argument. In what ways does the ego, by creating the need to be right, rob us of happiness? Debating the ego can be a minute-to-minute practice! Time and again, we need to reinforce for ourselves how we want to feel. The reason this is important is that we see evidence of what we believe. So if we believe we are unhappy, our brains will find lots of evidence to support this claim and hold us from feeling happy in response to what we see. If we believe we are happy, it will do the same.

Focusing on how you want to feel is an amazing paradigm shift for most people. Didn't we grow up in a "no pain, no gain" type of society? How many of you were raised as "good girls" and "good boys," based on how well you could conform? The subtle influence of that philosophy is "If I am hurting, exhausted, suffering, I am progressing in life. If I am uncomfortable, that is probably good. But if I am comfortable, I am probably being lazy or at least not working or living to my capacity." This paradigm is hurting people. We can feel good and happy about a job well done too. We can feel happy about a day off. We can feel happy about reading a good book or seeing a wonderful movie. We can feel happy about a nap! We can feel happy about virtually any element of our lives at any time.

Feeling good is a compass. Do more of what you love, put yourself in your life, and weed out the most frustrating aspects. Some of the frustration may be an inevitable part of a job or a relationship; however, in that case, we can turn to acceptance to release some of the suffering. When we accept, we stop resisting. We do not expect it to be different at every turn. Then we can turn our attention to our happiness rather than a focus on the frustration.

What makes you happy? Has anyone ever teased you about your happy place? My mother teases me all the time about the ocean. She knows I can be there dawn until dusk with my books, feeling the sand and sun, and listening to the ocean. She knows I get giddy at the prospect of going. She also knows that if I am going to the beach with people who spend too much time packing coolers and worrying about umbrellas, I become unhappy and eventually bolt with my beach bag to "save seats" for them to join me later!

Others can spend all day in the woods on hikes. Some people love the color purple and are happy when they see it. Some find Disney World the happiest place on earth. My husband is very happy on the golf course, on Wednesday nights at our trivia night, and the rare times he beats my brother-in-law at Words with Friends. So much happiness!

Take a few moments to think about what makes you happy. It is part of getting to know your true self. Are you ready for your own happiness? Are you ready to look around and make sure you see things that make you happy? Are you ready to ensure you make time for your own happiness? Of course you are! Let it flow.

CHAPTER 21

Mindfulness

"Look at other people and ask yourself if you are really seeing them or just your thoughts about them."
—Jon Kabat-Zinn

Mindfulness is the practice of observing the present moment nonjudgmentally. Repeat: nonjudgmentally! This is clearly a method to combat discontentedness.

Jon Kabat-Zin brought mindfulness to the West in the 1970s by creating a Mindfulness-Based Stress Reduction (MBSR) program to help patients with chronic pain. More recently, there has been a focus on teaching mindfulness in schools in programs like Goldie Hawn's MindUP. I teach mindfulness in the workplace and to clients and groups, as an approach to alleviate stress, at The Center.

Mindfulness challenges the ego to be present in the current moment without labeling it good or bad. As we do this, we mentally walk away from thoughts of the past or future and connect to the now. This allows us to reclaim time and energy from the not-now.

How does the not-now waste our time and energy? Here is an example: you think, "I have soooo much to worry about. There's my kids, the finances, my aging parents, my health, etc. etc.!" But the now is contained in the people and conversations around you, the work at hand. This is the now, and all of your worrying doesn't fix much.

Action might. If there are things to worry about and consider, move them to action. Find the right space and place to consider these worries. You may need to arrange a time to redirect worries into facing challenges. This is taking action against the fear (worry).

How often are you thinking of home when you are at work, and thinking of work when you are at home? Or do you worry about the end of vacation as soon as you get there? These are extremely common examples of mind*less*ness, and they present a wonderful opportunity to practice mindfulness! Try to focus on what is at hand. New studies are showing that multitasking is not a positive activity for our brains, and we are actually creating a trained distraction that damages our focus with constant task switching and the loss of momentum.

Find some present moments to observe this week. Take a mindful minute in the sun, or in your car. Or eat mindfully, tasting the food, noticing the texture, flavors, and aromas. Instead of answering e-mails, surfing the internet, watching TV, and eating at the same time, choose just one task to focus on. See if giving yourself permission to "single task" helps you develop a greater sense of contentment.

CHAPTER 22

Letting Go

"Some of us think holding on makes us strong,
but sometimes it is letting go."
—Hermann Hesse

I hear often, "I know I should let go, but how?" I say, "If you believe you should let go, you are 80 percent there!" The remaining 20 percent is in the doing.

We cannot keep collecting endlessly. As we become overloaded and overwhelmed, we may need to apply the concept of letting go literally and figuratively, with everything from grudges to furniture. Clearing the clutter can begin with letting go of things that are not valuable, but can also include letting go of useful or valuable possessions which may be difficult but necessary; we are sentimentally connected to many items. Instead of viewing it as throwing something away, release the item into the world for someone else to use. Even if it is something you cherish, if it no longer has a use for you, imagine that new owner loving and enjoying it. You can share it with the world and feel wonderful.

Several years ago, when my son Steven was sixteen years old, he wanted a gold cross necklace. I had a thought: "I have one for you," I said, and I went to my jewelry box and got out a gold cross necklace. I gave it to him and said, "This is your brother Jack's christening cross." It was a gift from Jack's godmother. Steve thanked me, and it was a special moment between the two of us.

A couple months later, the cross was lost in the boys' locker room and never returned. At first, it was like a punch in the stomach. I couldn't believe it was lost. Then I realized that not only was this a normal turn of events in a sixteen-year-old's life, but that as much as it was an extremely special gold cross, it was just a piece of jewelry. It was a thing. It was not Jack himself. Jack would not have been mad about it. Beyond this, I realized that perhaps Jack's christening cross ended up around the neck of someone who could use it. I imagined his cross landing with someone who needed a special gift and some significant inspiration and guidance. It made me feel happy and connected to Jack. The opportunity to show loving kindness to Steven was valuable as well. I was able to demonstrate to him that it was not something he should be ashamed of. It reinforced that he is more important to me than any piece of jewelry, even a sentimental one.

It still makes me feel good and close to Jack to share this story. It has become the symbol that the cross once was. After all, Jack is the inspiration for my shift to this career and, for that matter, this book too!

Relationships and what occurs within them can form some of the most hurtful examples of letting go. Sometimes people come into your life for a season. In a friendship that experiences a parting of ways, you may both need open capacity to welcome others into your life. It may not be forever, or it may be. Perhaps it is happening for a reason you do not understand.

Perhaps the letting-go challenge is forgiveness. I am sure you have heard that you are forgiving for you, not them. As the expression goes, "Not forgiving is drinking poison and hoping the other person dies." In forgiving, we release the person and in doing so release ourselves from the tether of pain. We are accepting what is, and also accepting the lesson in our lives.

There are many ways to make your letting go more real. You can have a letting go ceremony in which you write a letter to the person and the act you wish to forgive on paper and burn it. You can understand that thoughts of past are now just memories, and the thoughts that keep hurting you can be healed. One of our practitioners at The Center, Laura Normile, MA, offers a program called "Psychosomatic Journey," which teaches the healing of emotional wounds by addressing these thoughts and recreating new ones. You can also rewrite your story from a different perspective. You can visit your loved one before they passed away in your own thoughts when you didn't get a chance to do that in reality. You can say today what you would have liked to say then. You can speak the truth when you may have been silent. You can accept that a tragedy is part of your life's story rather than feeling it was a tragic accident. All are thoughts after a moment has passed.

Through emotional journeys and ceremonies, the writing of a new story, or just relaxing and releasing judgment, we can let go of that which holds us in a negative vibration.

CHAPTER 23

Living as Comparison-
& Judgment-Free
as Possible

"The root cause of all judgment is the fear
of not being good enough, not being worthy of love,
and not being safe."
—Gabrielle Bernstein

Comparing ourselves to others is a dysfunctional tool we use to measure our success. Authentic success requires that we set our own priorities, challenges, and values. Everyone's personal circumstance and life path is different, and unfavorable comparisons do not serve us. In order to have what someone else has, you must trade the whole lot, and unless you are living in a movie, you cannot.

Most of us walk a path of success and struggle. It is far too easy to see only the good in others' lives and not their obstacles, challenges, and pain. Think again of Facebook "boast" posts, or feeling self-conscious about your home, car, clothes, height, weight, or the size of your bank accounts. Comparisons are not necessary and they are hurtful, and they stand in the way of living our best lives. This can lead us to unfair self-judgment and criticism, which causes stress. It also creates blocks and fuels fear of pursuing what you would like to pursue.

Judgment is addictive. We get a slight fix from creating separation and feeling superior by judging another. But, once again, this is ego-created separation, and since we are all connected, the high is fleeting and the hangover hurts. Further, it goes against our nature. According to the wonderful book and six-step practice *Judgment Detox* by Gabrielle Bernstein, judgment makes us feel bad, as we are denying our true nature of oneness. We often judge to feel more worthy ourselves, because we have been less than kind to ourselves in our thoughts. We may also judge someone because he is doing something we may not allow ourselves to do, whether because of fear or conditioning.

When we judge someone as being not at all like us, we may actually be upset because that person is exhibiting a part of our own personality we do not like. We may feel irritated, aggravated, or frustrated around this person. Our feelings demonstrate resistance and provide an opportunity to learn more about *ourselves*.

What is it that challenges us so? To be truly free, we must drop judgment. Judgment is the ego's way of creating separateness. The ego is also often wrong when perceiving another's motives, acting on our own hurt and our own perspective without knowledge of what is real. Don Miguel Ruiz, in his book *The Four Agreements,* shares in the second agreement, "Don't Take Anything Personally," that everyone is operating from their own perspective. Even if that person is saying you are the problem, what they really mean is they have a problem with you and it is based on their beliefs, their experiences, and their judgments. If your friend is hurt by something you said and she calls you out on it, you can understand how she may have taken your statement and apologize, knowing that you did not intentionally hurt her and that her hurt is not your complete responsibility even in this given situation. You can witness your own defensiveness rather than sharing it and justifying your actions, accepting the pain of knowing you did hurt her feelings without ruminating on it.

Now that we have raised both unfavorable comparisons and judgments into your consciousness, a good rule of thumb is to notice them as they arise. Live as free as possible from these two forms of JOY ROBBERS! When you feel them cropping up in your thoughts, smile, tell yourself you are amazing and unique, and release the comparison or judgment as fast as you can!

CHAPTER 24

Joy

"Joy is the infallible sign of the presence of God."
—*Pierre Teilhard de Chardin*

In the *Book of Joy* by His Holiness the Dalai Lama, Archbishop Desmond Tutu, and Douglas Abrams, joy is described as more vast than happiness. I waited to mention this book till my final chapter, because at the end of *The Book of Joy* they have a chapter on joy practices. Lo and behold, it contains all of what we have discussed in our pillars! Meditation, compassion, perspective, acceptance, and gratitude are all in their book. They include obstacles to joy such as stress, suffering, loneliness, fear, anger, sadness, and envy. It brings me great happiness and, yes, JOY to open their book and find so much of what we advocate in our pillars as critical to cultivating joy!

When we acknowledge that stress and suffering need to be addressed in order to enable joy to shine through, it offers us a direction. If we wish to feel more joy in our lives, we must absolutely address our negative thoughts and feelings and how we approach suffering.

So, we have some work to do, but we also have some tools. In all of our chapters, we discuss ego. The ego certainly plays a role in prohibiting joy, as it is always looking for its next challenge, rather than connecting with spirit and others. Creating stress consciousness, becoming as comparison- and judgment-free as possible, moving from fear to love and scarcity to abundance clears the way as well. All of the previous chapters play a role in allowing joy to find us and live through us.

In thinking about what brings me joy, I came to some quick realizations. First, sharing clarity, compassion, and contentment with others in my work is an obvious joy. The only time it ceases to be joyful is when my ego starts to unfairly judge my success. When that happens, I get deflated in a hurry, and tired, exhausted, and self-doubting. When I return to a loving thought from fearful ones, I realize that I would be doing exactly what I am doing if you waved a magic wand and made all my dreams come true.

The Voice—I have to mention this show! *The Voice* brings me so much joy! This TV show is actually bigger than happiness for me. It sets off a vibration in me, a resonance at a deeper level, like bells and whistles going off on my insides. I get completely wrapped up in watching the contestants grow and the coaches coach. I find myself choked up at magnificent performances and wonderful interactions with coaches. I am rooting for them all. I want to punch my husband if he's watching with me and sarcastically says, "Was that supposed to be good?" or "Karaoke." (Like any good husband, he knows how to really get my goat! Luckily, he usually watches football in the other room.) Their newest coach, Kelly Clarkson, demonstrates so much joy that it has taken my enjoyment of the show to a whole new level! Note that they do not have judges on this show, but rather coaches. Of course this resonates with me!

Performing resonates with me too. Ever since I was a little girl, I've been performing. First, dancing and singing around the living room, dreaming of growing up to become Barbra Streisand, later entertaining older family members in songs and skits with my aunt, then performing as the prosecutor in two mock trials in high school. Unfortunately, and of great disappointment to me, I can't actually sing. Well, I can sing, just very poorly. Instead, I excel at public speaking. In adulthood, with family and friends and in social situations, I suppose there was a certain level of performance, but this has especially been the case in my career in public relations. I do like to be in front of an audience. I appreciate connecting to others from the stage.

So what else brings me joy?

My son and nephews bring me great joy. I feel a profound sense of purpose and joy in watching them all grow. Back when Jack and Steven were little, there was so much joy. Oh, there were temper tantrums, sleepless nights, and many loads of laundry too, but I remember those days as being filled with so much purpose, laughter, and awe. Here are a few of our joyful family-favorite stories.

When Jack was four, he was a reader. I had shared Hooked on Phonics with him, and he loved it. At the library book sale, I purchased a fifty-states textbook for him. He loved the book so much that he memorized all the state capitals and could recognize each state by its shape.

One day, as he was eating a slice of cheese, he put it was on the table. I looked at the chewed shape and said, "Jack, that looks like the United States!" I grabbed my camera and took a picture. In the photo he has a cheese-eating grin! About a year later, he was eating a Pop-Tart. You can see what's coming, right? I said, "Jack! Idaho!" and he yelled, "I know!" I took another picture. I brought the pictures in to work and my colleague said, "I'd like to see him try Hawaii."

When Jack was a little younger, around three, he finished his bath and changed into his pajama bottoms and T-shirt, but not his flannel pajama top. He was walking around, entertaining baby Stevie, and he said, "I'm freezin'!" I said "Come here, honey. I have your pajama top." He said, "I'm freezin'!" again, and I said, "Come here and I'll put your pajama top on!" My husband, Dave said, "Really? I'm actually a little warm myself." Jack said, "Want my shirt?" We burst into laughter as we realized he had his terms for hot and cold mixed up. We've told that story many times, with him in spirit.

The amazing thing is that when I am cold, the thought that pops into my head is "I am warm." I stop and think, "What?!" Then I say, "Hello, Jack."

The joy lives on. Jack gave me memories to last a lifetime. We just didn't consciously know I would need it.

Life is full of joy, and our heartbreak doesn't diminish it, but rather makes it more intense, if we only allow it.

What a beautiful place for me to end and for you to begin.

Start by asking yourself, How joyful are you? How joyful do you want to be?

What brings you joy?

_____

_____

_____

_____

_____

_____

_____

_____

_____

_____

_____

CHAPTER 25

What Is Next?

If you have enjoyed this book, I thank you from the bottom of my heart. Please know that you have brought me great joy! Thank you for helping me make the case for clarity, compassion, and contentment. If this has resonated with you and you are wondering "What is next?" here is what you can do.

1. Make sure you purchase *The Inspired Life Journal,* written by my business partner Helene Verdile and available on our website, center4c.com. Experience the joy of connecting with your higher self and taking time to move clarity, compassion, and contentment front and center in your life.

2. Join our monthly newsletter **mailing list** at center4c.com.

3. Make sure you follow our **programs** and **group coaching**, onsite and online, and let

us know if there is anything you would like to participate in, or if you would like a **free discovery session** to determine if **coaching** is something you find intriguing.

4. **Spread the message of clarity, compassion, and contentment.** Tell friends about the book, our Center, and coaching.

5. **Create a movement.** Consider joining a Center for Clarity, Compassion & Contentment Mastermind Group. This is a series of six sessions, online via video conference or in person, to discuss ways we can deepen our relationships at home and in our communities through the practice and demonstration of these pillars in our lives.

6. If you are interested in learning more about any of the authors I reference, consult the **Resources.**

7. One last thing! **Let me know if you are interested in a sequel.** There is so much more, and we have only just scratched the surface.

The deep dive into our inspired lives continues. . . .

Thank you!

If you would like to continue this conversation
(and I hope you do!), please contact me at

kperone@center4c.com

www.Center4C.com

Inspired Life Coaching at
The Center for Clarity, Compassion & Contentment

CHAPTER 26

Resources

Armstrong, Karen. *The Twelve Steps to a Compassionate Life.* New York: Albert A. Knopf, 2010.

Bernstein, Gabrielle. *Judgment Detox: Release the Beliefs That Hold You Back from Living a Better Life.* New York: North Star Way, 2018.

Brown, Brené. *The Gifts of Imperfection.* Minnesota: Hazelton Publishing, 2010.

Campbell, Joseph. *The Hero with a Thousand Faces.* New York: Pantheon Books, 1949.

Chödrön, Pema. *Fail, Fail Again, Fail Better: Wise Advice for Leaning into the Unknown.* Colorado: Sounds True, 2015

Dalai Lama, Archbishop Desmond Tutu, and Douglas Abrams, Douglas. *The Book of Joy.* New York: Avery, 2016.

Dyer, Dr. Wayne W. *Change Your Thoughts, Change Your Life*, California: Hay House, 2007.

Dyer, Dr. Wayne W. *I Can See Clearly Now.* California: Hay House, 2014.

Enneagram Institute, enneagraminstitute.com

Frankl, Viktor. *Man's Search for Meaning*. Massachusetts: Beacon Press, 1959.

Garden State. Directed by Zach Braff. Los Angeles, CA: Camelot Pictures, 2004.

Hanson, Rick, PhD. Rickhanson.net.

Harris, Dan. *10% Happier: How I Tamed the Voice in My Head, Reduced Stress Without Losing My Edge, and Found Self-Help That Actually Works—A True Story.* New York: Harper Collins, 2014.

Hawn, Goldie. Mindup.org.

Hay, Louise, and Robert Holden. *Life Loves You.* California: Hay House, 2015

Hay House Coach Camp with Robert Holden, Las Vegas, November 3–4, 2018.

Holden, Robert, PhD. *Shift Happens!: How to Live an Inspired Life . . . Right Now!* California: Hay House, 2011.

Ilibagiza, Immaculée. *Left to Tell: Discovering God Amidst the Rwandan Holocaust.* California: Hay House, 2006.

Kabat-Zinn PhD, Jon, *Full Catastrophe Living (Revised Edition: Using the Wisdom of Your body and Mind to Face Stress, Pain, and Illness.* New York: Random House Publishing Group, 2013.

Lewis, Scarlett and Natasha Stoynoff, *Nurturing Healing Love: A Mother's Journey of Hope and Forgiveness.* California: Hay House, 2013.

Maslow, Abraham H., *Motivation and Personality.* 2nd ed., Chapter 11 "Self-Actualizing People: A Study of Psychological Health"

Neff, Kristin, PhD. *Self-Compassion: The Proven Power of Being Kind to Yourself.* New York: Harper Collins, 2011.

Ruiz, don Miguel. *The Four Agreements*. California: Amber-Allen Publishing, Inc., 1997

Schucman, Helen. *A Course in Miracles*. Third Edition, California: Foundation for Inner Peace, 2007

Singer, Michael. *The Untethered Soul*. California: New Harbinger Publications, Inc., 2007

Steindl-Rast, David. Gratefulness.org.

Tolle, Eckhart. *A New Earth: Awakening to Your Life's Purpose*. New York: Penguin Books, 2005.

Tolle, Eckhart. *The Power of Now: A Guide to Spiritual Enlightenment*. California: New World Library, 1999.

Twist, Lynne. *The Soul of Money*. New York: W.W. Norton & Company, 2017.

Williamson, Marianne. *A Return to Love*. New York: Harper Collins, 1992.

Zukav, Gary. *The Seat of the Soul*. New York: Simon & Shuster, 1989.

Myers-Briggs Type Indicator,

https://www.myersbriggs.org/my-mbti-personality-type/

ACKNOWLEDGMENTS

With the deepest gratitude, I thank Helene Verdile for being a wonderful teacher, mentor, and business partner; plus my clients, Helene's clients, our workshop and seminar participants, special VIPs who champion us, and our practitioners at The Center. Specifically, I want to thank Elaine McDuffee and Brigitte Connors, because they are dear friends and were among the first two to grace our Center. I imagined them reading this book, and their warmth and appreciation for The Center kept me going despite any self-doubt. My editor Robin Catalano and cover designer Jennifer McDonald are magnificent! For all their support and love, I would like to thank my husband, Dave, and my children, Jack and Steven, as well as Helene's husband, Mike, and their children, Michaela, Julia, and Sam. Without them, there would be no Center. I have been blessed many times over and continue to work in JOY!

ABOUT THE AUTHOR

Kim Perone is a personal strategist, philosopher, and champion for her clients. After a twenty-year career in communication, public relations, and community relations, Kim trained as a life, success, and spiritual coach and opened Inspired Life Coaching practice and The Center for Clarity, Compassion & Contentment: A Wellness Center in 2015. With a strong belief in the individual and in inspired living, Kim continues her personal and professional path toward greater awareness, greater ability to serve clients and groups, and ever-greater spiritual knowledge. Kim helps clients achieve life balance, manage transitions, develop resilience, determine authentic success, and find their highest selves, all while navigating the choppy waters of modern life. She lives in Glenville, New York, with her husband, Dave.